Palm Beach
County

Pictorial Research by Fred L. Eckel
"Partners in Progress" by John P. Johnson

Produced in cooperation with the
Historical Society of Palm Beach County

Windsor Publications, Inc.
Northridge, California

Palm Beach County

An Illustrated History

Donald W. Curl

Windsor Publications, Inc.—History Books
  Division
Publisher: John M. Phillips
Editorial Director: Teri Davis Greenberg
Design Director: Alexander D'Anca

Staff for *Palm Beach County: An Illustrated
  History*
Senior Editor: Karl Stull
Assistant Editor: Marilyn Horn
Director, Corporate Biographies: Karen Story
Assistant Director, Corporate Biographies:
  Phyllis Gray
Editor, Corporate Biographies: Judith Hunter
Sales Representative, Corporate Biographies:
  Clive Bates
Editorial Assistants: Kathy M. Brown, Marcie
  Goldstein, Pat Pittman, Sharon L. Volz

Designer: J.R. Vasquez

Library of Congress
Cataloging-in-Publication Data

Curl, Donald Walter, 1935-
  Palm Beach County, an illustrated history.

  Bibliography: p.212
  Includes index.
  1. Palm Beach County (Fla.)—History. 2.
  Palm Beach County (Fla.)—Description and
  travel. 3. Palm Beach County (Fla.)—Industries. I. Eckel, Fred L. II. Historical Society
  of Palm Beach County (Fla.) III. Title.
  F317.P2C87   1986   975.9'32   86-9133
  ISBN 0-89781-167-4

Endpapers: *This scene of pioneer life in Palm Beach
County shows two typical lake sloops. Between the
boats, the two men seated under the cabbage and mastic
trees are "Cap" Dimick (left) and Robert Moore. The
camera is looking west across Lake Worth, circa 1890.
Courtesy, Historical Society of Palm Beach County
(HSPBC), Spencer Collection*

Title page: *The elite of American society gathered for
the winter season at Henry M. Flagler's two great resort
hotels, the Royal Poinciana and The Breakers. Shown at
the Royal Poinciana in 1896 are Colonel Philip Lydig
and Gladys Vanderbilt (sitting); Helen Morton (in veil),
Amy Townsend, Mrs. Cornelius Vanderbilt, and Mable
Gerry; Captain Rose and Edith Bishop (heads visible
only); Thomas Cushing, Edward Livingston, and Craig
Wadsworth; Gertrude Vanderbilt, Lispenard Stewart,
and Harry Payne Whitney. Courtesy, HSPBC*

Contents page: *The first steamboat to enter Lake
Worth, in February 1883, was drawn by George Wells
Potter, the area's earliest resident artist. He studied with
Kenyon Cox in Cincinnati, Ohio, before coming to south
Florida for his health in the early 1870s. Courtesy,
HSPBC*

Contents

Acknowledgments

No history project is completed in isolation. The aid, kindness, and good natured acceptance of many tedious requests on the part of many individuals made the research and writing of this work possible. I particularly wish to thank Mary C. Linehan, Judge James R. Knott, and Fred Eckel, who read the manuscript—sometimes more than once—and whose corrections, criticisms, and suggestions both kept me from many errors of fact and made the work much stronger. I also wish to thank Eunice Canty, Peggy McCall, and Anne Merrill of the Boca Raton Historical Society; Clorice Keats of the Boynton Beach Historical Society; Joan Runkel of the Henry Morrison Flagler Museum Archives; Becky Smith of the Historical Association of Southern Florida; and Maxine Banash, Jon von Gunst-Andersen, Alexandra Fatio Taylor, and especially Nan Dennison of the Historical Society of Palm Beach County, who gave hours of their time for the project. Bessie DuBois, who must know more about the history of Palm Beach County than everyone else put together, shared her knowledge, research, and photographs, and I thank her. Finally, Thelma Spangler typed the manuscript and, as usual, found and corrected many of my errors before I even noticed them. Her wisdom, and particularly her humor, probably made finishing the manuscript possible.

These two debonair cyclists are posing on a garden bridge on the Charles J. Clarke lakeside estate, Primavera. The man on the left is Louis Simpson Clarke. Courtesy, HSPBC

CHAPTER I

Jupiter Lighthouse, the area's chief landmark during the years of settlement, was photographed after its restoration in 1879 by Melville E. Spencer, an early resident whose camera preserved numerous scenes of Palm Beach County history. Courtesy, HSPBC, Spencer Collection

A Tropical Wilderness

*L*ate one afternoon in the autumn of 1872, young Charles Pierce accompanied his father to the top of the Jupiter Lighthouse to watch the keepers prepare the great lamp to warn mariners away from the dangerous off-shore reef. After the men had filled the oil tanks, cleaned and polished the large lenses, and wound and exactly timed the turning mechanism, the father and son went out onto the balcony to await the lighting of the lamp at sundown. From the top of the lighthouse, a panoramic view of south Florida spread before eight-year-old Charlie's eyes. Far to the south the sun's last rays seemed to dance on the gleaming surface of distant Lake Worth, which was surrounded by dense banks of dark green trees. Charlie could little dream that the silent and uninhabited land he surveyed—the most isolated region on the eastern coast of the United States—would, in just over two decades, become the nation's most renowned and fashionable winter resort.

Over the centuries many peoples had lived around the shores of Lake Worth. Ponce de Leon, who landed on the Florida coast in 1513, found several aboriginal Indian tribes inhabiting the area. Mounds built by these Indians show evidence of several closely related tribes having lived on the land that would become Palm Beach County. The Tequesta, a tribe that populated the seacoast as far south as Cape Sable, may have settled as far north as present-day Boca Raton. Farther to the north were the villages of the Jeaga. The Calusa, a people from the lower southwestern coast, probably lived around Lake Okeechobee.

John Hawkins' voyage up the Florida coast in about 1565 gives the earliest description of these Indians. His small English fleet sailed northward, investigating every inlet. The Indians he saw lived in large barn-like structures supported by the trunks of whole trees and covered with palmetto fronds. The diet of the coastal tribes, the Tequesta and Jeaga, consisted largely of oysters and other shellfish. The Indians' midden (refuse) mounds were later destroyed for the shells, which were used in road-building. The Indians who lived in the inland regions ate terrapins and other land turtles, and hunted deer and bear.

Above: *There are still stretches of the Loxahatchee River that give one a sense of the natural beauty beheld by the Indians and early settlers of Florida. Courtesy, HSPBC*

Right: *The Tequestas of southeastern Florida coastal areas were contemporaries of the Timucuan tribe seen by Jacques Le Moyne on his 1564 visit to the St. Johns River region. The dugout canoe is similar to the type used by the Seminoles three centuries later. Engraving by Theodore De Bry after a drawing by Le Moyne. From* The New World: The First Pictures of America *by Stefan Lorant*

Jonathan Dickinson, an English Quaker merchant, gave a brief description of life in a Jeaga village after the ship carrying him and his family from Jamaica to Philadelphia went down off Hobe Sound. Although everyone landed safely, they soon found themselves captives of the Jeaga "Casseekey" (cacique, or chief), who briefly held them prisoner at his village south of the Jupiter Inlet. Dickinson eventually reached Philadelphia, where in 1699 he published a journal that described his adventure.

These early Indian tribes had disappeared by the time the first settlers arrived in south Florida in the nineteenth century. Some succumbed to the diseases brought by Europeans to the New World. Some were taken as slaves. Others died in wars among Indian tribes and Spanish and English explorers. The rest left with the Spanish in 1763.

As the original native population declined, the Spanish sought new inhabitants for their large province, inviting the Seminoles as allies to come to Florida in the early eighteenth century. Originally members of the Creek tribes of Georgia and Alabama, the Seminoles ("wild ones") settled along the northern Florida border.

After Florida became a part of the United

GODS

PROTECTING PROVIDENCE
MAN'S
SUREST HELP AND DEFENCE
In the times
Of the greateſt difficulty and moſt Imminent danger;
Evidenced in the

Remarkable Deliverance

Of divers Perſons,
From the devouring Waves of the Sea, amongſt which
they Suffered Shipwrack.
And alſo
From the more cruelly devouring jawes of the inhumane
CANIBALS of FLORIDA.
Faithfully related by one of the perſons concerned therein;
JONATHAN DICKENSON.

Psal. 93 : 4. *The Lord on high is mightier than the noiſe of many Waters,
yea than the mighty Waves of the Sea.*
Psal. 74 : 20. *Thedark places of the Earth are full of the habitations
of Cruelty.*

Printed in *Philadelphia* by *Reinier Janſen.* 1699.

Left: *Jonathan Dickinson's book, a best-seller in colonial America, was the first published account of the land and inhabitants of the Palm Beach County area. From the 1975 reprint edited by E.W. and C.M. Andrews. Courtesy, Valentine Books, Stuart, FL*

Above: *On Christmas Day 1837, Colonel Zachary Taylor led 1,000 troops against 500 Indian warriors above the northeastern end of Lake Okeechobee. This was the Seminoles' last attempt to hold their ground in battle. Engraving by Gilbert and Gihon. Courtesy, HSPBC*

States in 1821, white settlers flooded into the area and forced the Seminoles to move southward down the peninsula. As the settlement continued, Floridians demanded that the Seminoles be relocated to reservations in the western part of the United States. The federal government ordered the Seminole chiefs to move their people to Indian Territory by January 1836.

In December 1835 several younger Seminole leaders decided to challenge this order. The young rebels ambushed and slaughtered Major Francis Langhorne Dade and two companies of soldiers. In all, 108 men were killed, and only 3 escaped. This massacre ushered in what became known as the Second Seminole War. (General Andrew Jackson's sortie into Spanish Florida in 1818 was called the First Seminole War.) In 1836 Florida created Dade County, naming it for the first white casualty.

Palm Beach County saw little action during

the conflict, though on Christmas Day in 1837 the fighting came close. The largest engagement of the war, called the Battle of Okeechobee, pitted more than 1,000 American soldiers against almost 500 Seminole Indians. Colonel Zachary Taylor, the future U.S. president, commanded the white forces while Sam Jones, one of the most feared of the Seminole warriors, led the Indians. Although outnumbered two-to-one, the Seminoles had their position well-prepared and inflicted many casualties. Only after Taylor ordered an attack on their flank did the Indians withdraw and escape to the east.

While Taylor came south through the middle of Florida, his commander, Major General Thomas S. Jesup, led his troops along the

Lake Worth is named for the last military commander of United States forces in the Second Seminole War, Colonel William Jenkins Worth, who declared the war over on August 14, 1842. Courtesy, HSPBC

coast. On January 24, 1838, Jesup met the enemy at the Battle of Lockahatchee. Once more the Indians inflicted a large number of casualties, even wounding Jesup before they disappeared into the wilderness. Nevertheless, by the end of the month Jesup had established Fort Jupiter. (In 1854 President Franklin Pierce would designate a portion of the reservation as the site for the Jupiter Lighthouse.) As an additional defense, Jesup also built a palisaded log fort on the bank of the Loxahatchee River.

On another front, Major William Lauderdale and his Tennessee Volunteers continued down the coast to the New River settlement and constructed a stockade, which Jesup named Fort Lauderdale. The route the Tennessee Volunteers hacked out through Palm Beach County, along the pine ridge separating the coastal swamps and the Everglades, became known as Military Trail.

Colonel William Jenkins Worth, receiving his appointment as commander in Florida in 1840, continued his predecessors' policies of pushing the enemy further south and shipping captives to Indian Territory. Two years later, on August 14, 1842, Worth declared the war over. The handful of Seminoles who remained in Florida agreed to occupy a temporary reservation at the southwestern tip of the peninsula, and although the Seminoles signed no formal peace treaty, the fighting came to an end. During Worth's tenure, his troops discovered the twenty-two-mile-long coastal lake that bears his name.

Homesteading in south Florida began in 1842 with congressional passage of the Armed Occupation Act. In a measure that preceded the Homestead Act by twenty years, Congress granted 160 acres of land to any family head who filed for and settled on the property. In *Early Lantana, Her Neighbors and More* Mary Collar Linehan identified twenty-one men who applied for claims around the shores of Lake Worth, although how many actually settled is unknown. One source says that a small group migrated to the lake country, but fled in 1849 when four outcast Seminoles killed one of their number while he was tending his fields. None of this group remained by 1872.

In that year the Jupiter Lighthouse was already twelve years old. In March 1853 Congress appropriated $35,000 to build a lighthouse at the Jupiter Inlet near the junction of the Loxahatchee and Indian rivers. George Gordon Meade, who later commanded the Army of the Potomac at the Battle of Gettysburg, designed the new lighthouse.

The uninhabited site presented numerous construction difficulties. The Jupiter Inlet filled with silt, forcing the builders to haul materials by barge thirty-five miles downstream from the Indian River Inlet. Mosquitoes and sand flies in addition to the extreme heat made life miserable for the workers. Then, shortly after construction had started, a party of surveyors destroyed the garden of Billy Bowlegs, an Indian leader, thereby igniting the Third Seminole War. The hostilities halted construction of the lighthouse until the last years of the decade. Finally, on July 10, 1860, the great lantern flashed its light for the first time.

In less than a year the nation was plunged into the Civil War. Supporters of the South believed that the lighthouse aided the Union in maintaining its naval blockade. Among those demanding that the lighthouse be shut down was August Oswald Lang, the assistant keeper. With the help of two other Southern sympathizers he removed and hid part of the light's mechanism. The men justified their action to Florida Governor M.S. Perry by asserting that the light was "of no use or benefit to our government, but on the contrary, of great importance to our enemies."

During the war years Captain James Arango Armour served as a volunteer coastal pilot for the Union patrol boat *Sagamore*. Originally from New York City, and an ardent supporter of the Union, he came to the Indian River area in the late 1850s and quickly learned the south Florida waterways. Under his pilotage, the *Sagamore* caught many blockade runners attempting to supply the Confederacy from the Bahamas.

At the end of the war, Armour found the missing parts of the Jupiter light, and when it once again flashed over the Atlantic on June 28, 1866, he had become assistant keeper. Just three years later, in 1869, Armour began his thirty-six-year service as head keeper at Jupiter. When Armour married Almeda Catherine

Born in 1825, James Arango Armour came to the Titusville area in the 1850s. During the Civil War he served as pilot on the U.S.S. Sagamore, *which maintained the Union blockade in southeast Florida. After the war he signed on as an assistant keeper at Jupiter, and from 1867 to 1908 he was the keeper of the Jupiter Lighthouse. Courtesy, HSPBC*

Carlile in December 1867 and brought her to Jupiter Lighthouse, no other white woman lived within 100 miles. On November 16, 1868, their daughter, Kathernine Dickerson Armour, became the first white child born in Palm Beach County.

During the 1870s and 1880s almost everyone going south to the lake country stopped at the lighthouse, including the generation of pioneers who eventually settled Palm Beach County. During this period, several of Armour's assis-

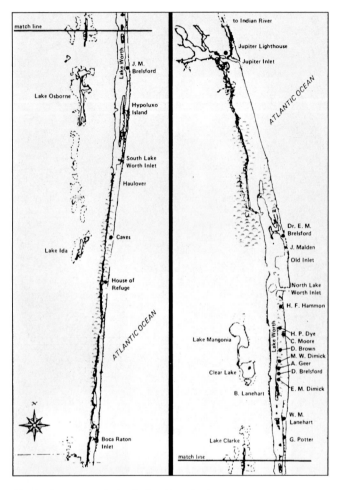

Early homesteads in Palm Beach County are shown in two panels, with the north at the right and the south continued at the left. Map by Mrs. Robert Powell. From Pioneer Life in Southeast Florida *by Charles W. Pierce*

tants became homesteaders on the lake, among them Charlie's father, Hannibal Dillingham Pierce.

The first resident of the lake country was August Lang, the former assistant keeper who had disabled the light to aid the Confederacy. Perhaps fearing arrest by the crews of the coastal patrols, he had moved to the lake during the Civil War. Afterward he settled in the Indian River area. In 1870, when Dr. John Milton Hawkes traveled down the east coast from Jacksonville to Miami, he hired Lang as a guide. In a brief travelog on Florida published the next year, Hawkes mentioned spending a night near Lang's abandoned Lake Worth house to "replenish [supplies] from his four-acre potato patch, which was running wild."

In November 1872, an old sailor named Charles Moore became the second settler on the lake, taking over Lang's cabin. Jesse Malden and his wife arrived soon after and stayed on, though originally Malden came to the lake to hunt and fish and had no plans to homestead.

William M. Butler arrived next. He built a small ten-by-twelve-foot cabin on an island near the south end of the lake and collected local fauna specimens for the University of Rochester in New York. He shared his cabin with newcomer William H. Moore, the brother of Charlie's mother, Margretta Moore Pierce. The Pierces, who came to Florida because of Moore's poor health, followed. H.D. Pierce cleared a cabin site about a mile south of Butler's. He found timbers for the frame of his house scattered along the beach and used palmetto fronds for the roof and walls.

Shortly after the Pierces settled into their new house, a party of Indians arrived at the island. Margretta Pierce asked one of them the Seminole name for the lake. The Indian replied, "Hypoluxo," saying it meant "water all around, no get out." As the lake already had an English name, the new settlers decided to call their island Hypoluxo.

Early in the winter of 1873 Hiram F. Hammon and William M. Lanehart arrived on the lake to take up homesteads. During a visit the year before, Hammon found that the climate eased his crippling rheumatism. He formally entered the area's first homestead claim on July 28, 1873. H.D. Pierce filed the second on May 26, 1874, claiming 50.19 acres on Hypoluxo Island.

In December 1874 Captain Harlan Page Dye brought Mason M. Dwight to the lake.

Dwight, who was searching for a new home for his wife, young son, and father, a retired clergyman, selected a site about a quarter of a mile south of Charles Moore's property. On returning to Jacksonville, he chartered a boat to bring building supplies, citrus trees, and other provisions. William Lanehart built the Dwights' house, the first large and well-furnished dwelling on the lake. Nonetheless, it had a palmetto-frond roof in the style of the other early structures.

After a south Florida summer, spent fighting mosquitoes and suffering from the heat, the Dwights decided to return north and in early June 1876 sold their property to David E. Brown and his family. The Dwights had brought a widow with two grown children, Mrs. E.J. Wilder, to serve as their cook. When Charles Moore learned that the Dwights planned to leave he asked Mrs. Wilder to be his bride. The ceremony, performed by Mason Dwight's father in his son's living room, was the first on the lake.

The summer of 1876 also brought the Dimicks from Constantine, Michigan. The family included two brothers, Elisha Newton (known as "Cap") Dimick and Franklin L. Dimick; their parents; their sister Marion and her husband Albert Geer; and a number of children. The schooner carrying their household goods and building materials was unable to navigate the shallow inlet, so they had to land their be-

Left: *The residence of the Hannibal D. Pierce family in the 1870s and 1880s was the second homestead on Hypoluxo Island and only the fifth on the twenty miles of Lake Worth in 1872. Photo by Melville E. Spencer. Courtesy, HSPBC, Spencer Collection*

Above: *Four visiting Seminoles were photographed at Jupiter Lighthouse in 1879 by Melville E. Spencer. From left to right, they were Doctor's Boy, (unknown), Robert Osceola, and Little Tyger. Courtesy, HSPBC, Spencer Collection*

Above: *While many homesteaders established successful farms, all benefited by the vast natural bounty of the region, still evident in this Loxahatchee view, circa 1920. Photo by Ernest Histed. Courtesy, HSPBC*

Facing page: The *Oh Kim Soon, stranded at Point Manalapan in 1897, was one of many sailing ships that fell victim to the Florida Straits. Cargo washed ashore provided a good living to hundreds of settlers during the nineteenth century. Courtesy, Bessie Wilson DuBois Collection*

longings by small boat and ferry the heavy cargo to shore by raft.

Most of the early settlers came to the lake country to farm. Although the climatic conditions of tropical Florida created some problems at first, the farmers soon found the rich virgin muck and the red-hammock lands highly productive. They experimented with many crops. Sweet potatoes and Indian pumpkins grew to bumper yields, which continued to reseed themselves year after year.

In 1879 the settlers planted about 15,000 pineapple slips. Cultivating pineapples proved to be extremely hard work, though for a number of years splendid harvests provided good profits. Eventually the fields gave out and a blight hit the crops. Then the price fell consid-

erably, as Caribbean pineapples entered the American market after 1912. The extreme hard work and reduced profits combined to persuade most pineapple farmers to try other cash crops.

In the early 1890s pioneer farmers earned most of their income by growing vegetables for the northern winter market. Although they produced tomatoes, beans, eggplants, melons, and strawberries in abundance, it remained a precarious business until the coming of the railroad. Even then, because of wind conditions, the first large tomato harvest rotted before it could be sailed to the railhead.

While the early settlers searched for a cash crop, most lived almost entirely from the natural bounty of the land. Deer, wild ducks and turkeys, quail, and a large variety of fish allowed the pioneers to be nearly self-sufficient, though some staples such as flour and coffee

had to be purchased.

In the earliest years they beachcombed for copper, brass, tin, and lead to provide a stake at the general store. Copper brought fifteen cents a pound, and brass, tin, and lead earned five cents. Because the closest general store was at Sand Point (later named Titusville), and a round trip meant sailing for over 300 miles on both ocean and inland waters in a small boat, the pioneers were lucky that 400 or 500 pounds of scrap metal paid for supplies for several months.

Over the years the Florida reef had taken a large and tragic toll of ships. The sandy beach enabled most shipwreck victims to reach the shore safely. Their peril lay in finding no shelter, food, or water along the nearly deserted coastline. In 1873 a United States Life Saving Service report recommended that five houses of refuge, each manned by a keeper, be construct-

Above: *Orange Grove House of Refuge No. 3, located on the beach ridge a few hundred yards north of present-day Atlantic Avenue in Delray Beach, was built in 1876 as a haven for shipwreck survivors. The first keeper was Hannibal D. Pierce, who moved his family seven miles south to the Orange Grove House from their lonely Hypoluxo Island homestead. Courtesy, HSPBC*

Right: *This palmetto-frond hut was built with the assistance of Melville E. Spencer, who then took the photograph on May 9, 1876. Benjamin Lanehart is the man holding the gun; Abner Wilder stands in the door. Courtesy, HSPBC, Spencer Collection*

ed at Bethel Creek, Saint Lucie Rocks (Gilbert's Bar), Orange Grove, Fort Lauderdale, and at the head of Biscayne Bay. Congress approved the plan in June 1874, and construction on the $2,900 houses began immediately. Each house was exactly alike; the first floor served as the keeper's home, the second as a temporary dormitory for shipwreck survivors.

Like many of the settlers on the lake, H.D. Pierce had no secure source of income. So, in the spring of 1876, when he learned that a keeper was needed for the House of Refuge some five miles down the beach from the lake, he applied. Pierce's application was accepted for the $400-a-year post, and in April the family moved to the newly completed house at Orange Grove.

At the Pierces' new home (officially known as Orange Grove House of Refuge No. 3), on August 15, 1876, Margretta Pierce gave birth to their daughter Lillie Elder. Pierce remained as keeper for more than a year, and resigned in May 1877. His replacement, a young man from England named Stephen Andrews, held the job until the station closed in 1893.

Melville Evans Spencer, another early homesteader, worked for six years as assistant keeper of the Jupiter Lighthouse, putting his earnings into the improvement of his lake property. He had come from northeastern Pennsylvania in the spring of 1876 and taken up 123 acres of oceanfront land. Eighteen months later his parents, Mr. and Mrs. Valorus Orlando Spencer, and his two sisters, Flora and Martha (Mattie), arrived.

In 1879 Captain U.D. Hendrickson, a young man from Cleveland, Ohio, began making regular trips from Lake Worth to Titusville in his newly built New Haven-type sharpie, *Illinois.* For the first time, the settlers had regular transportation to and from the outside world.

Hendrickson hauled crops and passengers to the Indian River town and brought needed supplies and new settlers back to the lake.

By 1880 the lake settlers believed their numbers warranted regular mail service from the U.S. government. A route had been established along the southeast coast of Florida in 1850 but was discontinued in September 1869. Throughout the 1870s, those living at Jupiter or on the lake received mail only when a trustworthy traveler passed through. On January 13, 1880, V.O. Spencer and his daughter Mattie sailed around the lake collecting signatures on a petition that requested that the old route be reopened. Although their boat capsized on the trip home, Mattie saved the petition by securing it in a wooden box.

On May 30, 1880, the Post Office Department ordered that the route be reestablished and named V.O. Spencer postmaster of Lake Worth, Florida. At the time, the name "Lake Worth" applied to the entire lake area. The mail came by boat down the Indian River to Jupiter. From there, the carrier walked to the head of Lake Worth and sailed the last few miles down to the post office, which Spencer maintained in his own house.

With the start of regular freight and passenger service to Titusville, and the opening of a scheduled mail route, the early settlers on the lake began to feel closer to the outside world. They had accomplished the most vital and dangerous tasks of pioneering, and now they were ready to establish those institutions that signal the emergence of civilization.

The sharpie-class sailboat was considered a fine form of Lake Worth transportation. The Heron, shown in this 1893 photograph, was built by William Lanehart for owners George W. Potter and Vincent Gilpin. Courtesy, HSPBC

CHAPTER II

This scene of pioneer life in Palm Beach County shows two typical lake sloops. Between the boats, the two men seated under the cabbage and mastic trees are "Cap" Dimick (left) and Robert Moore. The camera is looking west across Lake Worth, circa 1890. Courtesy, HSPBC, Spencer Collection

Lake Country Pioneers

Over the next thirteen years, 1880 to 1893, the isolated and primitive life of the earliest settlers gave way to relative convenience: scheduled transportation by boats, stagecoach, and even railroad, an organized school and church, well-stocked general stores, and comfortable hotels for tourists seeking the magic of summer during the winter. Along with a steady increase in the permanent population, this era also saw the first of the seasonal residents who built large, modern houses along the lakefront.

In the summer of 1885, the Post Office Department created a mail route from Lake Worth to Biscayne Bay. Because there were no roads to Miami, the new route meant a sixty-mile walk down the ocean beach. To speed the trip, the carrier kept to the hard-packed wet sand near the water's edge, and to save his shoes from the salt water he walked barefoot. Theodore Pratt first called this the "barefoot route" in his 1943 novel *The Barefoot Mailman.*

Edwin Ruthven Bradley received the first $600-a-year contract to carry the mail to Miami. A former newspaper reporter from Chicago, he and his family came to the lake in 1877 and took up a homestead on the west shore near its southern end. Bradley shared the carrier duties with his sixteen-year-old son Louis. Every Monday one of them left the lake on their three-day trip to Miami. The first night, the carrier stayed at the Orange Grove House of Refuge, just five miles to the south. On Tuesday he walked twenty-five miles to the New River House of Refuge at Fort Lauderdale. He kept a boat to cross the Hillsboro Inlet, and another to cross the New River. On Wednesday morning the mailman continued ten miles down the beach to the head of Biscayne Bay. Here he kept a third boat to cross the bay to Miami. Thursday morning he began the trip home and returned to the lake about noon on Saturday.

Although the barefoot mailman sometimes took along "foot passengers" at five dollars a head, the job remained monotonous and lonely. By the early summer of 1887, the Bradleys decided that the $600-a-year salary failed to compensate for the tedious weekly trips and turned the route over to James Edward Hamilton, one of the "Kentucky boys."

During the pioneer era the sighting of a steamboat was a notable event, signaling the arrival of supplies, household goods, or new settlers in the area. Photo by Melville E. Spencer. Courtesy, HSPBC, Spencer Collection

Three young men from Trigg County, Kentucky—Hamilton, Andrew Walton Garnett, and James L. Porter—had arrived two years before, each purchasing six acres on the west shore of the lake, across from the Pierce homestead. Garnett served as postmaster when the new office at Hypoluxo was approved by Washington on May 18, 1886. His friend Ed Hamilton was less fortunate in the employ of the Post Office Department.

After lunch on Monday, October 10, 1887, Hamilton left on his weekly route to Miami. He spent that night at the Orange Grove House of Refuge. The keeper, Steve Andrews, mentioned that a beach bum had passed on his way to Miami the day before. Andrews warned the transient against using the mail carrier's skiff at the Hillsboro Inlet.

After Hamilton left the House of Refuge the next morning, he was never seen again. When he failed to return on Friday night, Andrews walked down to the Hillsboro Inlet. He found Hamilton's haversack with the special lightweight canvas mail pouch still inside and his shirt and pants hanging from a tree. He found the carrier's underwear on the bank of the inlet and saw the skiff tied up on the opposite bank.

Apparently the beach bum had taken the mail carrier's boat to the far side of the inlet. When Hamilton attempted to swim across to retrieve it, he either drowned (the heavy autumn rains left the water level quite high) or was attacked by sharks or alligators. A few days later Charles Pierce searched the inlet with his friend Louis Bradley. The young men saw a great number of alligators and concluded "that they played a sinister part in Hamilton's disappearance." Several parties searched the inlet but failed to find any trace of Hamilton.

After Hamilton's disappearance Andrew Garnett and Charles Pierce shared the duties of the barefoot route for about a year. The government continued the service with several additional mailmen until 1893. Henry John Burkhardt, the last of the barefoot mailmen, lost his job when a new road from the south end of the lake to Lemon City allowed a springless wagon to carry the mail.

Edmund Munger Brelsford and his brother, John H. Brelsford, came to the lake in the summer of 1881 from Xenia, Ohio. They purchased land from Frank Dimick and bought the schooner *Bessie B.* Opening a route between the lake and Jacksonville, they brought new settlers to the community and supplies for the general store, which they established in 1884.

The residents around the Brelsfords' store, more than a mile south of the Lake Worth post office, believed they deserved better mail service, and on January 15, 1887, President Grover Cleveland appointed E.M. Brelsford postmaster of Palm City, a name inspired by the many coconut trees on the island.

These trees, now almost a decade old, were descendants of a cargo of coconuts from the Spanish brig *Providencia,* bound for Cadiz from the island of Trinidad, which wrecked on January 9, 1878. It came ashore near the homesteads of Hiram Hammon and William Lanehart, who reached the scene first and claimed that before his rescue by a passing steamer, the captain of the *Providencia* had given them the ship and its contents. Although they charged two-and-a-half cents apiece, almost everyone on the lake bought and planted some coconuts.

In August postal authorities informed Brelsford that another Palm City already existed in Florida and that he must choose a new name. He wrote a letter back to the department that same month, saying it was the "unanimous wish of the entire community" that Palm Beach be the new designation. In a few years Palm Beach had displaced Lake Worth as the name for the entire lake country.

Washington approved the Figulus post office

Top: *Shooting sharks near Jupiter Inlet was one of the early sporting entertainments among rough and ready pioneers. Photo by Melville E. Spencer. Courtesy, HSPBC, Spencer Collection*

Bottom: *Sketches by George W. Potter accented the rustic appeal of the tropics to fashionable pioneers of the late 1880s. Four more of his drawings appear on the next page. Courtesy, HSPBC*

Pioneer-era artist George W. Potter was also a surveyor, lumber dealer, and founding partner of the first real estate firm in the lake country, Porter and Potter. Courtesy, HSPBC

on January 7, 1886. The word *figulus* is Latin for potter. The postmaster was Benjamin M. Potter, younger brother of early pioneers Dr. Richard B. Potter and George Wells Potter. The older brothers first reached Miami in January 1874 from Cincinnati, Ohio. Richard was a graduate of the Medical College of Ohio; George came to Florida because of his severe asthmatic condition. The brothers

initially claimed a homestead in northwest Miami. Richard practiced medicine and served as collector of customs and clerk of the Dade County courts.

By 1881, having faced several medical crises, settlers around the lake resolved to find a doctor for their community. They made overtures to Richard, who saw that the rapid growth of the area could support a practice. Although Richard remained on the bay until 1882 to prove his 170-acre claim, George moved to the lake and in 1881 homesteaded 160 acres on the beach ridge.

In 1882 Richard followed, as did their mother Lydia Ames Potter, a sister Ellen, and their younger brother Ben. In addition to farming his homestead, George, who had once been a cartoonist for the *Cincinnati Enquirer*, provided

drawings for Dr. James A. Henshall's *Camping and Cruising in Florida,* published in 1884.

The first of the prosperous winter residents was Denver businessman Robert R. McCormick, who bought Albert Geer's land in 1886 for the remarkable sum of $10,000. This was Palm Beach's first large real estate deal, and it caused considerable excitement around the lake. McCormick built a large house on the lakefront. A contemporary description called the grounds a "bower of elegance and tropical splendor," and the house their "crowning glory." Soon, Charles I. Cragin of Philadelphia, C. Vanderbilt Barton of New York, and Chicago Mayor George B. Swift joined the list of wealthy families who built large, seasonal houses on the lakefront.

Some of the original settlers left the area because they found the prospect of trying to make a living as farmers too hard and uncertain. Cap Dimick was determined to stay, though not as a farmer. In the summer of 1880, he added eight rooms to his house and

In 1880 Elisha N. "Cap" Dimick added eight rooms to his house for winter visitors. The Cocoanut Grove House became the center for resort activity in the decade before the arrival of Henry Morrison Flagler. In 1892 Charles J. Clarke bought the establishment, which burned down the following year. Courtesy, HSPBC

opened Palm Beach's first hotel, the Cocoanut Grove House. The hotel became both a mecca for winter tourists and a social center for the year-round residents.

During the winter of 1891-1892, Charles J. Clarke of Pittsburgh sailed his yacht down to Palm Beach. After a short visit, he fell in love with the area and decided to buy land. Dimick, having built onto his hotel several times while catering to the whims of numerous guests for twelve seasons, sold the building and sixty acres of ocean-to-lake land property to Clarke.

Captain Dye, too, opened a hotel on the lake. He had already begun a regular passenger service to and from Jacksonville in 1881 with his schooner *Gazelle,* and the next year he

Above: *Appointed as the first state circuit judge for Dade County in 1886, Allen E. Heyser remained the only resident judge for close to a quarter century. He settled on the west side of Lake Worth in 1885. His home, the Riviera Inn, was the namesake of the town of Riviera Beach. When the Dade county court moved back to Miami to 1899, so did he. Courtesy, HSPBC*

Right: *The white-bearded gentleman is Elbridge Gale, a professor of horticulture who retired to the west side of Lake Worth in 1884. He grew this Mulgoba mango tree from seeds sent by the U.S. Department of Agriculture. Seeds from this tree were used to produce the first Haden mango—an improved variety—on his homestead located six blocks north of Currie Park in present-day Mangonia. Courtesy, HSPBC*

opened the first grocery store in the Lake Worth village. Dye's ten-room hotel, constructed in 1884, burned down later the same year. In 1886 he built an even larger hotel of sixty-three rooms, which he called the Lake Worth.

Allen Edgar Heyser, originally from Pennsylvania, studied law in Georgia before coming to the lake in 1880. Shortly afterward, Governor William D. Bloxham appointed him county judge. At the time Heyser was the only judge in Dade County, and the only attorney. In 1885 he married Mattie Spencer, V.O. Spencer's daughter. He built the third hotel on the lake, the twenty-room Oak Lawn House. In 1893 Heyser changed the name of his hotel and the post office, which had been established four years earlier, to Riviera.

The Reverend Elbridge Gale, retiring in 1884 after a long career as professor of horticulture at the Kansas State Agriculture College, took up land south of the Heysers. Continuing his horticultural studies, he became interested in tropical plants. In 1889 Dr. David Fairchild, founder of Miami's Fairchild Garden and one of Gale's former students, gave him several mango trees, which had been imported from India. The Mulgoba variety proved to be

the most popular and became the ancestor to the well-known Haden strain.

Gale's daughter Hattie became the first schoolteacher in the lake country. In 1886 the county commissioners agreed to pay a teacher's salary if the families would build and equip a schoolhouse. Several settlers donated land, a subscription drive raised money for lumber, and volunteer labor finished the simple one-room building in time for school to open in March 1886. During the first term, sixteen-year-old Hattie taught students who ranged in age from six to seventeen.

After they established a school, many residents began to feel the need to organize a church. The Episcopal Bishop of Florida, visiting the lake and holding services during the winter of 1887-1888, decided the community could support a mission church. Reverend Joseph N. Mulford of Troy, New York, volunteered to become vicar during the winter months. Beginning on January 5, 1889, he held regular services in the schoolhouse. Shortly af-

Opening in March 1886, this was the first school in Dade County, which at that time included all of Broward and Palm Beach. This 1888 picture shows Miss Hattie Gale, the first schoolteacher (standing in the door in a white dress). On the far right is Guy Bradley, later shot in the line of duty as the first game warden in the Everglades in 1905. Photo by Melville E. Spencer. Courtesy, HSPBC, Spencer Collection

terward, Charles C. Haight, an architect and contractor who lived close to the school, built a small wooden church, which he finished in April. The vicar's wife, Mary Cluett Mulford, named the church Bethesda-by-the-Sea because her family attended Bethesda church in Saratoga Springs, New York, during the summer.

The congregation soon outgrew their little building. The first Bethesda church cost $600. Reverend Mulford had helped with the carpentry work. The second Bethesda church building, completed in 1895, cost more than $13,000. Mary Mulford said the architects designed a Moorish-style church adapted for Florida's climate.

Construction of docks at Jupiter Inlet made it possible for deep-water vessels to unload cargo for shipment via rail line to Lake Worth. On Lake Worth, shallow-draft sloops provided the main means of transport. Courtesy, HSPBC

Until 1909, when the state legislature created Palm Beach County, the southeast coast of Florida was all part of Dade County, and by the late 1880s the growing population around the lake had come to resent the sixty- to seventy-mile walk down the beach to the county seat in Miami. Parties to litigation, witnesses, those summoned for jury duty, applicants for marriage licenses, and others having legal business found themselves forced to make the long journey. A campaign by the citizens of the lake country resulted in a February 19, 1889, election to decide on a new location for the county seat.

The winner was a small settlement at the head of Lake Worth called Juno. A road built in 1885 from Jupiter had made Juno the distribution center for goods coming down the Indian River. In addition, by 1889, the Indian River Steamboat Company had started construction of the Jupiter and Lake Worth Railroad. Juno's victory was assured when Albert M. Field, a county commissioner and Juno homesteader, promised to donate a square-acre of land for the new county courthouse.

The north county easily outvoted the south,

In another view of Jupiter Inlet, circa 1890, a steamboat is moored at the northside dock. In the foreground is the southside dock of the Jupiter and Lake Worth Railroad pier. Courtesy, Bessie Wilson DuBois Collection

107 to 80. When the commission officially announced the returns, several angry Miami residents pledged to use force to retain the county seat in their town. As a result of the bitterness between the two regions, three "husky young men" were selected to bring the county records from Miami. To avoid a direct confrontation with the Miami locals, the records were loaded in the dark of night into a large Indian canoe and taken to New River by the Everglades route.

Authorizing construction of the new courthouse in February 1890, the commissioners awarded a $1,495 contract to C.C. Haight. The solidly built, thirty-by-thirty-five-foot, two-story frame structure, only a half-mile from

the head of the lake, soon became a sailor's landmark. The entire second floor was used for the courtroom. When court was not in session, the county often rented the room to church groups and fraternal organizations.

The courthouse attracted many new settlers to the area. In 1892 C.C. Chillingworth be-

came the county's second attorney. Originally from New York, Chillingworth graduated from Cornell and then studied law in Atlanta. He later recalled that although the "hamlet" of Juno had seven dwellings, two boardinghouses, a store, a newspaper building, a railway station, and the courthouse and jail, it never had a church, a preacher, a doctor, or a bank.

The promoters of the little town of Juno knew that completion of the railroad was vital. Although work on the roadbed had begun in October 1880, the slow delivery of rails (owing to limited cargo space on the steamers from Titusville) delayed the line's official opening until the summer of 1890. The three-foot-wide, narrow-gauge rolling stock came from the St. Johns and Halifax Railroad, which had been rebuilt to broad-gauge. Steamboats brought a wood-burning engine ("Old No. 3"), one passenger car, and three freight cars to Jupiter. A second passenger car, purchased in 1891, and perhaps a replacement engine made up the line's entire rolling stock.

For its time the Jupiter and Lake Worth Railroad charged high fares. Passengers paid ten cents a mile, or seventy-five cents, for a one-way trip. Because the line had no turntable, the train went forward to Juno and then backward to Jupiter. From the beginning, the old equipment was subject to frequent breakdowns. Nonetheless, Blus Reis, the jovial engineer, helped maintain good relations with the passengers. He often played "Dixie" on the engine's steam whistle while his passengers sang along.

In 1893 Julian Ralph published an article in

The Jupiter and Lake Worth, nicknamed the "Celestial Railroad," was the only rail line in southeast Florida before the Flagler era. The train traveled a narrow-gauge seven-and-a-half-mile track, facing forward as it went south but chugging backwards on the return trip north. Courtesy, Bessie Wilson DuBois Collection

XVI CENTURY

"SEARCH FOR THE TR

[THE INDIAN RIVER NEWS. Established Feb. 24, 1887.
Consolidated with THE TROPICAL SUN, M.h 18, 1891.]

MELBOURNE MENTION.

Mr. N. Downey was a visitor at the county seat last week, on legal business.

Our nurseryman, Mr. John B. Beach is shipping Queen pine-slips to California.

Capt. J. J. Fox and family are now back to their summer cottage on the

NOTES FROM OUR NEIG

South of Us—Miami, Lemon City Biscayne Bay, Cocoanut Grove

Mr. M. Dearborn started for last night, where he will await th al of the schooner "Hardee" an join the party for Biscayne, Bay he has taken up a homestead. ville Star, July 23.

Messrs. Charlie Christian, J. and J. McAllister start for Bisc day in the sloop "Enterprise"

Harper's Monthly in which he noted that the little railway from Jupiter to Juno also stopped for passengers at Mars and Venus. He dubbed the line the Celestial Railroad, and the nickname caught on.

The little railroad's most profitable period, though, foretold its end. Henry M. Flagler attempted to buy the line in 1893 but thought the asking price was too high. He decided instead to extend the tracks of his Florida East Coast Railway. However, until his railroad could reach the area, Flagler needed the services of the line to haul materials for his new hotel. For eight months the little train carried an immense amount of freight, charging Flagler an estimated $68,000. But, by February 1894, Flagler's railroad had bypassed Juno and made the little Jupiter and Lake Worth completely obsolete. The rolling stock of the now-bankrupt line was sold at public auction in June 1896.

At its height as the county seat, Juno brought southeast Florida its first newspaper. Guy I. Metcalf had been publishing the *Indian River News* in Melbourne since 1887. Many people on the lake wanted a newspaper to help promote their community, so when Melville Spencer offered to erect a new building for Metcalf, he agreed to move the newspaper to Juno. The two-story, twenty-by-forty-foot frame building contained a printing room, with solid cement bases for the presses, a room for the editors and reporters, and a small private office for Metcalf, all on the first floor. The editor and his staff lived on the second floor.

Metcalf needed a new name for the newspaper, and Judge Heyser suggested the *Tropical Sun,* which the editor adopted, though some readers insisted on calling it the "Prodigal Son." One of the first editorials called for the opening of a road to the Biscayne Bay country. Metcalf received the county contract in the spring of 1892 for a low bid of $24.50 a mile. By December the road was completed. Running from Lantana at the south end of the lake

to Lemon City, a small settlement north of Miami, it eliminated the need for the barefoot route down the beach.

Metcalf then successfully bid on the contract for a new mail route to run along his just-completed road. The vehicles used to transport mail were two "springless wagons covered with canvas." Metcalf brought his cousin, Frank Stranahan, down from Melbourne to operate the halfway camp he had established at the ferry on the New River. Stranahan thus became the original settler and founder of Fort Lauderdale.

Juno remained the county seat for only ten years. By 1899 the growth of Miami and other towns around Biscayne Bay had far outstripped the lake country. Five years before the county government left Juno, Guy Metcalf appraised the outlook for the town, sensed a troubled fu-

TROPICAL SUN

Avacado Pears   Lemons, Limes, Oranges, Mangos, Guavas, Bananas.   XIX CENTURY

...TH IS THE NOBLEST OCCUPATION OF MAN; ITS PUBLICATION A DUTY."

JUNO, DADE COUNTY, FLORIDA,   JULY 29, 1891.   VOL. V --- NO

HERE AND THERE.

Scraps of News About This and That And Different Things.

Mr. Fred Church, our County Sheriff, has moved his family and effects over to his new home near "Uncle Jimmie" Kinsley's farm.

Mrs. Ruby Moore returned yesterday from a pleasant visit to Cocoa, and is again at her duties on the staff of THE TROPICAL SUN.

Capt. George Sears and family start to-day for a three week's cruise on In-...

We are glad to see Charlie Converse, an old-time Melbourne boy, holding down the pursership on the St. Augustine.

The lake schooners "Mary B" and "Emily B" have both arrived in port and discharged cargo. The "Mary B" will be laid up a few weeks for repairs. The "Emily B" with Capt. Dave McLardy in command has started out again on her return trip to Jacksonville. This trip she will bring the lumber for the new houses to be built by Mr N. W. Pitts and by Mr Will Whidden, at Juno.

Notice to Mariners.

Florida.—Off Cape Canaveral.—Ohio Shoal.—New Buoy.—Buoy moved.—An iron spar buoy, painted black, has been placed on the eastern edge of Ohio Shoal, in 3½ fathoms of water, Cape Canaveral light bearing S. W. 3-4 S., distant 11⅛ miles.

The whistling buoy to the eastward of the shoal is now painted red, and lies in 11 fathoms of water, in a position from which the same light bears S. W. ½ S., distant 15 7-8 miles. L. H. Board, June 4, 2891. This affects Charts 161, 13, 14, and B.

OUR COCOA CORN...

Society Salad, Town Talk and For Our Cocoa Reade...

O. K. Wood returned las... from his pineapple farm at...

Last Monday was the hott... the season, the mercury 9..° in the shade.

Capt. James Knight a... Canaveral, were visitors i... several days last week-

Misses Rosser and Egg...

ture, and moved the *Tropical Sun* to the new town of West Palm Beach. After the closing of the railroad and the relocation of the newspaper and the county seat, few people remained to witness the forest fire that swept into Juno and destroyed what was left of the once prosperous village.

By 1893, the pioneer period around the shores of Lake Worth had ended. Telegraph lines, connecting boat and train schedules, and even a weekly newspaper all brought the residents of the lake country more and more into touch with the outside world. Even more importantly, the outside world had discovered Palm Beach.

The Tropical Sun, *a two-man weekly, was founded in Titusville in 1887 as the* Indian River News. *It moved in 1889 to Juno, the new Dade County seat, where it was renamed, and in 1893 it moved again to West Palm Beach. Guy Metcalf, the first editor, was mainly responsible for the first road from Lake Worth to Biscayne Bay in 1892. He also compaigned for the formation of a new county in north Dade, which in 1909 became Palm Beach County. Courtesy, HSPBC*

CHAPTER III

*Enjoying the resort life of 1907 are Mr. and Mrs.
William K. Vanderbilt, Jr. (he holding the alligator,
she seated), and, continuing left to right, Leland Sterry,
manager of The Breakers Hotel; Lawrence Waterbury;
and Fred Sterry, manager of the Royal Poinciana Hotel.
Photo by Ernest Histed. Courtesy, HSPBC*

Henry Morrison Flagler

When Henry Morrison Flagler visited Palm Beach in March 1892, he found several thriving little communities along the shores of Lake Worth. After only three days in the lush tropical setting, he decided to build a large resort hotel and to extend his railroad to the lake country. Flagler's development on the island made Palm Beach the nation's premier winter resort.

Flagler first visited Florida in the winter of 1878 because of his ailing first wife, Mary Harkness Flagler. They enjoyed Jacksonville and Saint Augustine, and Mary's health seemed to improve. Nonetheless, business made it impossible for Flagler to return to Florida the following year, and Mary refused to make the long difficult trip, which involved changes of trains and long delays, without him.

Mary Flagler, who had been a semi-invalid for seventeen years, died on May 18, 1881. In June 1883 Flagler married Ida Alice Shourds, a thirty-five-year-old practical nurse who had cared for Mary. They delayed their Florida honeymoon until December. Both delighted in the balmy weather, while the North suffered a prolonged cold spell. They stayed in Saint Augustine until March.

Flagler, an early partner of John D. Rockefeller, now played a less active role in the management of Standard Oil and was able to return to Florida the following February for the winter season. The Flaglers traveled in their new private railway car, the "Alicia," taking advantage of new tracks and scheduling to make the trip in only forty-eight hours. Flagler deplored the lack of first-class accommodations at Saint Augustine. He believed the "Ancient City" had great potential as a winter resort. After attending a celebration commemorating the landing of Ponce de Leon, he purchased land to build a luxury resort hotel.

To design the hotel, Flagler chose Thomas Hastings, a Paris-trained architect and the son of the pastor of Flagler's church. Hastings and John M. Carrere, another young architect, formed a partnership to accept the commission. Flagler, having decided to call his hotel the Ponce de Leon, asked for a Spanish-style building. One observer said the architects envisioned "a pleasure palace, embodying the characteris-

Henry M. Flagler was the person most responsible for the development of the east coast of Florida from 1885 to 1913. One of four founding partners in the Standard Oil Company, he made Palm Beach a fashionable resort. Courtesy, Henry Morrison Flagler Museum

tics of Spanish Renaissance architecture, with sunny courts and cool retreats, fountains, and towers, and decorations suggestive of the history of the city." The contractors James A. McGuire and Joseph E. McDonald completed the $2.5-million building in time for the opening on January 10, 1888.

By then all Pullman vestibule trains were making the New York City-to-Jacksonville run in twenty-nine hours. From Jacksonville, continuing to Saint Augustine, travelers crossed the Saint Johns River by ferry and boarded the narrow-gauge Jacksonville, Saint Augustine, and Halifax River Railroad. The thirty-mile trip often took most of a day. Late in 1885 Flagler bought this short line and immediately modernized the road, converting the track to standard gauge. During the next few years, he purchased the Saint Augustine and Palatka Railroad, the Saint Johns Railroad, and a lumbering line that took him all the way south to Daytona. Each railroad he acquired was converted to standard gauge and integrated into the new system.

On January 20, 1890, Flagler opened a new bridge across the Saint Johns River, making it possible to board in New York City and travel nonstop all the way down to Saint Augustine. The Ponce de Leon proved so successful that Flagler commissioned Carrere and Hastings to design a second hotel, which was called the Alcazar. Later he purchased the Casa Monica, which he renamed the Cordova, and connected it to the Alcazar. In 1890 Flagler also purchased the Ormond Beach Hotel, which he enlarged and "beautified." As his holdings in railroads and hotels grew, Flagler came to be regarded more and more as Florida's east coast empire builder.

Until 1892 Flagler built no new railroads, contenting himself with buying and modernizing existing lines. In that year he obtained a charter from the State of Florida, which authorized him to extend his line as far south as

Miami. At first, he seemed to feel that a connection with the Indian River steamers at Rockledge or Melbourne would complete his southward expansion. In fact, he renamed his new system the Jacksonville, Saint Augustine and Indian River Railroad. Flagler's March 1892 visit to Palm Beach greatly relieved the citizens of the lake country, who feared that the line would stop short of their community.

Flagler's visit to Lake Worth set off the area's first land boom. He ordered his land agent, Albert Robert, to purchase acreage on both sides of the lake. Robert bought R.R. McCormick's land for $75,000 and the northern part of the Brelsford property for $50,000. With Flagler willing to pay premium prices, excited landowners found that almost any

Sea Gull Cottage, built in 1885 for Robert R. McCormick of Denver, was the finest residence in Palm Beach when Flagler bought it in April 1893. It served as Flagler's home until Whitehall was completed in 1902. Afterward it was moved across the island for use as a rental cottage beside The Breakers. In 1984, it was moved back to the lakeside and restored to its former glory by the Preservation Foundation. Courtesy, HSPBC

property could find a buyer. Land that the pioneers had homesteaded, or purchased at very low prices, suddenly became worth $150 to $1,000 an acre.

On the west side of the lake, Flagler spent $45,000 to purchase land from two pioneer settlers, Captain O.S. Porter and Louis Hillhouse. This parcel of real estate became the town site of West Palm Beach. From the beginning, Flagler planned to build a commercial city on the west side of the lake. Although later the legend grew that he founded the town for servants and staff, Flagler in fact wanted to keep all commercial activities separated from the planned resort in Palm Beach, reserving its pristine tropical setting for the tourists.

In May 1892 McGuire and McDonald began building Flagler's hotel, the Royal Poinciana. Almost all the labor used in its construction was brought to the area by the contractors. To house the workers, a tent and shack community known as "the Styx" grew up north of the hotel site.

Legend also claims that Flagler ordered the Styx burned down while its residents were attending a circus in West Palm Beach. Casting some doubt on this dramatic version of events, Inez Pepper Lovett, who was an infant when her family moved to the Styx during the mid-1890s, recalled that the owners of the land, seeing how valuable it had become, simply ordered the residents, many of them blacks from the Bahamas, to move out. In an interview published in the *Palm Beach Post* Lovett said, "Maybe they did burn the shacks, but if they did, it was after everyone had already moved away." The land then became one of Palm Beach's earliest subdivisions.

The Royal Poinciana opened on February 11, 1894, with seventeen guests. The original hotel had 540 rooms. Although skeptics questioned

The spectacular results of Flagler's initial development are evident in these circa 1930 photographs. In the larger aerial view (facing page), The Breakers stands in the foreground, and to its left is the bathing casino (see smaller aerial for detail). This was the third version of The Breakers, built after a 1925 fire. The new lobby reflected the 1920s taste for elegance, while the main dining room retained the grand scale of the early wooden hotels.

Across the island from The Breakers, left to right, are the Whitehall Hotel, the Royal Poinciana, and the Alba Hotel. Across the lake, West Palm Beach has emerged as a city. Courtesy, HSPBC

Flagler's ability to entice that many guests into the wilderness of south Florida, the hotel proved popular from the very first. In 1899 and 1901 Flagler built large additions to the Royal Poinciana, which ultimately covered thirty-two acres. It was advertised as the largest wooden resort hotel in the world. Three miles of corridors led to 1,081 rooms that could accommodate 1,750 guests. The immense H-shaped dining room seated 1,600 patrons, served by 400 waiters. The headwaiter had twenty-six assistants and his own secretary.

A luxury suite cost $100 a day, which by 1890 standards was extremely expensive. Nonetheless, a small room on the top floor, without a bath, could be had for only six dollars. Discreetly concealed in every room was a gold-trimmed white china chamberpot decorated inside and out with green palm trees.

White and green characterized the interior of the hotel. Thick green matting imported from Japan cushioned the floors, green-and-white-patterned wallpaper covered the walls, and green-and-white wicker chairs furnished the rooms.

The exteriors of all of Flagler's wooden hotels were painted a vivid lemon yellow, as were his railway stations. This color became known as "Flagler yellow." The Royal Poinciana was once described as "a perfect barracks of a place," though "not at all an unattractive building from the architect's standpoint." In architecture, it was distantly related to the Georgian style, with green shutters, Corinthian-columned porches, and a tall tower.

The hotel opened before the railroad reached the lake. Although workers completed the tracks in late March, the first train did not arrive till April 2, 1894. Guests of the hotel had to be ferried across Lake Worth until 1895, when Flagler built a bridge for railroad and pedestrian traffic. The train tracks crossed the lake just to the south of the Royal Poinciana and continued across the island to the end of a

new steel pier, where Flagler's Palm Beach-Nassau Steamship Line offered regular service aboard the *Northumberland.*

By 1896 the Royal Poinciana had proved so popular that Flagler constructed a second hotel, called the Palm Beach Inn, on the oceanfront. Flagler remodeled and added more rooms to the Palm Beach Inn during the next four years and in 1900 changed its name to The Breakers. In 1903 fire completely destroyed the L-shaped four-story frame structure. A much larger U-shaped five-story building, completed in 1904, prospered as one of Flagler's most popular hotels.

During this period Flagler suffered a personal tragedy. In the fall of 1895, Alice Flagler had been committed to a private asylum for mental illness, after she announced her engagement to the Czar of Russia, with whom she claimed to communicate via her Ouija board. Although at times her condition seemed to improve, in August 1899 a New York court ruled her insane. By this time Flagler had not seen his wife in more than two years. As his biographer says, "to him Alice Flagler existed no more." However, New York law did not accept insanity as a basis for divorce.

In 1899 Flagler became a legal resident of Palm Beach. Two years later Florida passed legislation making incurable insanity grounds for dissolution of a marriage. Soon dubbed the "Flagler Divorce Law," it caused a furor, as newspapers accused him of buying the state legislature.

Flagler seemed to take no notice of the criticism. On August 13, 1901, he divorced Alice in the Circuit Court of Dade County. On August 21 the seventy-one-year-old millionaire announced his engagement to thirty-four-year-old Mary Lily Kenan of North Carolina. They were married three days later at the bride's family home in Kenansville, North Carolina.

As a wedding gift Flagler built Whitehall, the $2.5-million, white-marble mansion on

Henry Flagler's wedding present to Mary Lily Kenan was the grandest house in town, Whitehall, which today is the Henry Morrison Flagler Museum. Courtesy, Henry Morrison Flagler Museum

the lakeshore of Palm Beach. Designed by Carrere and Hastings and built by McGuire and McDonald, the town's largest house was completed for the 1902 season. Soon after moving in, Mary Lily complained of the noise from the trains that crossed the lake. The next year, Flagler relocated the railroad bridge to the north of the Royal Poinciana. The new route ended at a small depot on the west side of the island. From then on, transportation to the oceanfront hotel and casino was provided by a mule-drawn trolley.

Flagler's hotels attracted America's financial and social elite. The sidings beyond the new train station sometimes contained as many as sixty "palace" railway cars, the pre-aviation equivalent of a private jet. On one occasion, Harry Payne Whitney chartered a train for a party of twenty-five, taking over an entire floor

Alligator Joe and his pets resided near the lake at present-day Worth Avenue, where their business was to attract tourists during the first decade of the twentieth century. Courtesy, HSPBC

of one wing of the Royal Poinciana. In the early years, the guest lists often included the names of Vanderbilts, Belmonts, Astors, Goulds, and Stotesburys. The Palm Beach season, from around New Year's Day to February 22, became a prominent item on fashionable America's resort calendar.

So that his guests could be assured of all the most modern conveniences, Flagler paid for a new water plant, which also served the community, a new electrical generator, which supplied the first electric lights in south Florida, and a telephone switchboard, which served over 1,600

Colonel Edward Riley Bradley was widely respected in Palm Beach as a sportsman, churchman, and public-spirited resident for nearly half a century. His Idle Hour Farm in Lexington, Kentucky, like his Beach Club, combined a respectable business with betting activity. The lady on his left is Miss Beatrice MacGuire, a distant relation. Photo by Bert Morgan. Courtesy, HSPBC

telephones. Nevertheless a typical day in the resort could be exhausting, especially for female guests, because of the constant changing of clothes. The regimen—beginning with breakfast and proceeding to morning on the beach, lunch, afternoon sightseeing, the tea dance at the Cocoanut Grove, and finally dinner—called for at least seven different costumes.

The American plan was standard at Flagler's establishments. Nonetheless, many skipped the dinner provided by the hotel. Even with a ratio of one waiter to every four diners, Royal Poinciana guests complained that "the physical difficulties . . . in so huge an establishment"

meant a dish often arrived at the table cold.

No one ever complained of cold food at Bradley's Beach Club. Colonel Edward Riley Bradley, a gambler and owner of the Idle Hour Farm racing stable, opened the Bacchus Club, a gambling casino, in the early 1890s in Saint Augustine. By the end of the decade he and his

Bradley's Beach Club stood on the north side of Royal Poinciana Way where Bradley Place intersects it. From 1898 to 1945, everyone knew that the purpose of this institution was not corrupting local morals but entertaining out-of-state visitors. Although it was a gambling casino, it was the most respectable illegal enterprise in the state. Courtesy, HSPBC

brother John Bradley decided to follow their clientele to Palm Beach. In 1898 they constructed an unpretentious white frame building on the lakefront, about 1,000 feet north of the Royal Poinciana Hotel, which they incorporated under the laws of Florida as the private Beach Club.

When the club opened in the 1899 season, business was so bad that the brothers decided to close the casino and return to Saint Augustine. The story is told that several women asked if they might try their luck at the tables. Colonel Bradley said no. While women gambled in Europe, it had never been permitted in an American casino. John Bradley asked, "Oh, well, why not? We're closing up, so what's the difference?"

According to this story, the next night every

lady of fashion in Palm Beach descended upon the club, assuring its success. Bradley's became known for the high stakes at its roulette, faro, and English hazzard tables and for the fine food on its dining tables. Although gambling was illegal in Florida, the club operated for almost fifty years, closing only in 1945, a year before Colonel Bradley's death.

Why did Florida permit Bradley's to continue? Perhaps state officials feared that tourists would go elsewhere if Palm Beach had no casino. In any case, many people thought of the island as a world apart from the rest of Florida and gladly embraced the fiction that the casino accepted no Floridians as members, although Thomas Reese, the club secretary, has said he admitted many local businessmen and residents. The most compelling reason to ignore gambling in the club probably stemmed from the choice of membership, which in Reese's words comprised people with "plenty of money and no squawks at losing." Bradley insisted on perfect decorum at all times within the club. Then, too, Colonel Bradley always contributed generously to local charities, churches (he was a major patron of Saint Edward's Catholic Church in Palm Beach), and political campaigns.

Across the lake, West Palm Beach had its beginnings in August 1893, when Flagler's surveyors laid out the mainland townsite, which extended west to Clear Lake. The streets were named in alphabetical order, after trees, fruits, and flowers that grew in the area. Running east and west were Althea, Banyan, Clematis, Datura, Evernia, and Fern streets. The north-south avenues were Lantana, Narcissus, Olive, Poinsettia, Rosemary, Sapodilla, and Tamarind. As the Royal Poinciana neared completion, all the streets within three blocks of the lakefront were cleared, graded, and paved with crushed oyster shells from the Loxahatchee River. On February 4, 1894, an auction was held in the ballroom of the Royal Poinciana to sell the first lots in the new town.

Many of the purchasers were workers who had come to Palm Beach to build the hotel, living with their families in tents, thatched shacks, or hastily constructed boardinghouses on the hotel grounds. Flagler, who understood the continuing need for skilled artisans, wished them to remain in the area. He also wanted the shacks and tents off the hotel grounds.

The new community was built rapidly as the first property owners used their savings and skills to construct houses and business buildings. At the same time, some former workers simply moved their tents and shacks across the lake and, in the words of one report, seemed "inclined to disregard the rights of their fellows." By fall the more public-spirited element of the community decided to incorporate as a municipality, in order to gain the authority to curb the excesses of the less public-spirited element.

A meeting of the registered voters—held on November 5, 1894, in "the town hall over the Calaboose"—voted to incorporate, choosing the name "West Palm Beach" rather than "Flagler," which had also been suggested. The same group also elected the first officers for the new municipality: John S. Earman, mayor; Eli Sims, clerk; W.L. Tolbert, marshal; and George W. Potter, E.H. Dimick, J.M. Garland, J.F. Lamond, George Zapf, H.T. Grant, and H.J. Burkhardt, aldermen. The aldermen met two days later and named Potter as their chairman.

At the end of 1895, the town's first year, a census showed a population of 1,928 persons and property valued at $133,926. For the next few years, town government continued to be conducted in the room over the calaboose (this small jail had been built by the railroad in cooperation with the county, because the closest jail was miles away in Juno). Among the chief concerns faced by the first town council was the hard surfacing of the principal thoroughfares. Although crushed oyster shells proved a satisfactory pavement for light vehicles, heavier traffic produced large potholes that required constant attention. To solve the problem, city engineer Franklin Sheen discontinued use of the shells, substituting coquina rock.

As early as March 1895 the council decided to put before the voters a $25,000 bond issue to construct sewers and provide for fire protection. The proposal met so much opposition that the election was delayed until August. Although the measure was finally approved, the town could attract no buyers and so never sold the issue.

Since West Palm Beach did not establish its own fire department, a volunteer company known as the Flagler Alerts handled firefighting duties on both sides of the lake. Organized in November 1894, the volunteers had to manage without much equipment. Henry Flagler donated a hand-operated pumper; the town installed a few hydrants and bought 500 feet of hose.

Like many a frontier settlement, West Palm Beach had a notorious district, Banyan Street. One of the original aldermen, George Zapf, numbered among the saloon owners. By law saloons in West Palm Beach had to close from twelve midnight to four-thirty and all day Sunday. The saloon owners of Banyan Street petitioned the council to allow them to remain open twenty-four hours a day, seven days a week. But, with only one marshal in town, the law could only rarely be enforced on the street, which also flaunted open gambling and ladies of easy virtue.

In 1895 Sam Lewis, a bartender, became the area's first lynching victim. During a Banyan Street poker game, he argued with and later shot the county tax collector and another man. Lewis also killed a young deputy sheriff before being captured by a posse and taken to the Juno jail. The senseless killings so outraged the community that on the night of August 24 a mob stormed the jail. After hanging Lewis

from a telegraph pole, the mob riddled his body with bullets.

A counterbalance to the Banyan Street saloons came in the form of the many churches built in West Palm Beach. The first was Union Congregation Church, officially organized on March 25, 1894, on Easter Sunday. Its building, on a Flagler-donated site at Olive Avenue and Datura Street, was dedicated on July 24 of the same year. Other churches quickly followed. Saint Ann's Catholic Church also received its lot from Flagler, who financed the cost of moving the small white chapel a few blocks to the Olive Avenue site. Holy Trinity Episcopal Church and a Methodist church were founded before the end of the century, as were the first two black churches of West Palm Beach: Tabernacle Missionary Baptist and Payne Chapel African Methodist Episcopal. The town council gave twenty-five dollars toward the purchase of the Methodist church's bell, which the fire department also used for an alarm.

The town received electric and telephone service before the end of the century. Electricity cost a dollar-and-a-half per month for business lights and sixty cents for each light in a private house, no matter how much current was used. In 1898 W.S. Boynton and M.B. Lyman received a temporary permit to operate a telephone "plant." In 1899 the council gave John B. Beach and George S. Adams a twenty-five-year franchise for telephone service, but they were succeeded in 1904 by a company that established a modern telephone exchange. The

Flagler in a jovial mood is seen here with Joseph Jefferson (left) and Senator Chauncey M. Depew of New York (center). Jefferson was a famous actor in nineteenth-century America who owned a home in Palm Beach and spent a good deal of his retirement there. Courtesy, HSPBC

The high school in West Palm Beach was the largest educational edifice in southeast Florida when it was built in 1908. It still stands on the Twin Lakes campus, though without the upper half of the main tower. Courtesy, HSPBC

directors included Beach, M.E. Gruber, Dr. J.E. Liddy, and J.R. Anthony, Jr.

In 1896 two fires struck the business district. The town council immediately enacted a new building code calling for the use of stone, brick, or brick veneer in all downtown construction. Within months a flurry of rebuilding had transformed the little town into a city of real substance and permanence. An 1896 directory and guide for Dade County listed 135 places of business in West Palm Beach.

In 1903 the council decided to ask the Florida legislature to grant a city charter. C.C. Chillingworth and his law partner George Currie handled the legal aspects of the change, and on July 21, 1903, council president George Potter

The Breakers (top), rebuilt after a 1903 fire, and the Royal Poinciana were first and foremost during the hotel era of Palm Beach. Courtesy, HSPBC

*A typical day at the resort included a morning visit to
the beach or the bathing casino of The Breakers, a lakeside promenade, teatime at the Cocoanut Grove, and
perhaps a visit to Alligator Joe's Pavilion. Courtesy,
HSPBC*

Facing page: *A stroll through the grounds of the Royal Poinciana offered views of Whitehall and the Royal Poinciana Chapel. Courtesy, Henry Morrison Flagler Museum; HSPBC*

Joseph Jefferson, shown in a moment of ease, was active in the civic and commercial development of early West Palm Beach. Courtesy, HSPBC

Above: *Clematis Avenue, shown circa 1910 on the preceding page, changed in the years after the war as West Palm Beach grew from a frontier town to cityhood. Courtesy, HSPBC*

Facing page: *After World War I the hotels gave way as centers of resort life to exclusive clubs, such as the Bath and Tennis Club and the Everglades Club. Paintings by Joseph Webster Golinkin. Courtesy, Chisholm Gallery, Palm Beach Polo and Country Club at Wellington*

The transition from the Flagler era to the palacio era was reflected in the style of fashionable houses, as the simplicity of Sunset Avenue was succeeded by the grandeur of the James P. Donahue residence. Courtesy, HSPBC

announced that West Palm Beach had officially become a city.

One of the city's most distinguished early investors and benefactors was Joseph Jefferson, an actor known especially for his role of Rip Van Winkle. Jefferson contributed liberally to many local causes, including the fire department. He built the West Palm Beach Electric Light, Ice, and Power Company. As a land developer he erected a modern hotel and several houses and laid out a twenty-acre residential subdivision known as Jefferson's Lake View Extension just south of the downtown area. When he died in Palm Beach in April 1905, the West Palm Beach Board of Trade, on which he had served as honorary chairman, voted to suspend all business the next day. Every storeowner in town, "including the Syrian merchants and Wo Kee, the Chinaman," agreed to the closing.

A group of Palm Beach businessmen organized the first bank in the lake country with backing from James R. Pritchard of Titusville. The Dade County State Bank opened in a small frame building on May 1, 1893, the same day construction started on the Royal Poinciana Hotel. Edmund and John Brelsford, George Lainhart, Cap Dimick, and Captain Hendrickson served as local officers and directors. In 1895 the bank purchased property at Clematis Avenue and Olive Street for a West Palm Beach branch. That same year an amended charter authorized transfer of all operations—and the bank building—to the new town on the west side of the lake. In 1899 a new two-story brick building was completed. During the next year the Potter brothers and their sister Ellen bought the controlling stock of the Titusville banker. The name Dade County State Bank was changed to Pioneer Bank after the founding of Palm Beach County.

On May 10, 1899, Miami vied with Juno once again to become the seat of Dade County, winning the election 690 to 468. As reflected in the tally of votes, the south end of the county had experienced rapid growth, which accelerated in 1894-1895 when Flagler decided to extend the railroad to Biscayne Bay and to construct a large resort hotel on the banks of the Miami River. As the railroad built south from West Palm Beach, new communities sprang up along its route, including Boynton, Linton (later Delray Beach), and Boca Raton.

After the loss of the county seat to Miami, Guy Metcalf began a campaign in the *Tropical Sun* for the formation of a new county with the city of West Palm Beach as its governmental center. This campaign bore fruit in 1909 when the Florida legislature created Palm Beach County from the north end of Dade. Since West Palm Beach had recently built a modern $50,000 school, on a hilltop site west of downtown donated by Ellen Potter, the old city school at Clematis Avenue and Poinsettia Street (Dixie Highway) became the county courthouse.

The new city of West Palm Beach had come into its own as the commercial center of the new county of Palm Beach. Across the lake, a new era would soon begin in the capital of fashionable America's winter resort life.

CHAPTER IV

A new flamboyance was evident in Palm Beach society after World War I, exemplified by Prince Mdivani and fiancee Louise VanAlen. Courtesy, HSPBC

Playground of the Elite

wo luxury hotels established Palm Beach
the winter capital of American high society.
over two decades the nation's leaders of
nce and fashion registered at either the
yal Poinciana or The Breakers for the early-
uary to February 22 season. Since their
y was so short, few resorters maintained
ses in town. Those who did usually followed
example of the earliest residents in building
dest frame-and-shingle cottages along the
shore. This pattern of resort life changed
pletely after World War I. The season be-
he longer and longer, as society gave up the
els and built imposing mansions in Mediter-
ean-Revival styles. The most luxurious of
new villas faced the ocean.

he person most responsible for the transfor-
ion of Palm Beach resort life was Paris
ger, one of four sons and two daughters of
c M. Singer, the sewing machine magnate,
Isabella Singer, his last wife. Paris Singer,
was born in the French capital and spent
t of his life in Europe, inherited an im-
se fortune on his father's death. When
rld War I broke out, he converted his two

French estates and one in England into military hospitals. He then decided to come to the
United States.

Shortly after arriving in New York Singer
met Addison Mizner, a genial society architect
with a Long Island country house practice.
Singer's interest in architecture and Mizner's
outgoing personality and wit helped cement an
almost instant friendship. Since the coming of
the war had ended Mizner's architectural commissions, Singer invited the architect to spend
the winter season with him in his Palm Beach
villa. Mizner, who was convalescing slowly after
being injured by hitchhikers during a robbery
attempt, welcomed the move. An extremely
cold winter had hampered his recovery, setting
off fears he might lose his leg.

Singer was accustomed to a more active life
than that of the Florida resort—he had only
recently ended an almost decade-long tempes-
tuous affair with Isadora Duncan, the danc-
er—and soon became bored with the daily
routines of the Palm Beach season. A meeting
with *Touchstone Magazine* editor Mary Fanton
Roberts, who used her publication to educate

Above: *Paris Singer, a son of sewing-machine magnate Isaac Singer, was a guiding spirit in the Palm Beach of the 1920s, founding the Everglades Club and bringing architect Addison Mizner to the resort. Courtesy, HSPBC*

Right: *Addison Mizner was an architect in New York City for twelve years before moving to Palm Beach in January 1918. His success in adapting the Spanish-Mediterranean-Revival style to the resort life of Palm Beach County brought a new era to south Florida. Here he is seen conferring with two from his famous menagerie of pet parrots and monkeys. Courtesy, HSPBC*

American women on the problems faced by shell-shocked soldiers returning to civilian life, led Singer to propose building a convalescent hospital for these victims in Palm Beach.

From the first Singer anticipated that when the war ended and the need for a hospital had passed, it would become a private club, a more exclusive alternative to resort social life than the public hotels. As Mizner had recovered under the influence of the Florida sun, Singer asked him to design the hospital and to direct the Ocean and Lake Realty Company, which

The success of the Everglades Club coincided with a lengthening of the social season and a trend toward a greater informality than was permitted in the hotels. Courtesy, HSPBC

he established to manage his many Palm Beach land purchases.

The architect came from a prominent California family. His father, Lansing Bond Mizner, a land developer, attorney, and Republican politician, served as United States minister to the five Central American republics under President Benjamin Harrison. The young and impressionable sixteen-year-old Addison accompanied his father in the spring of 1889 to Guatemala City where the United States maintained its diplomatic residence and offices. Although Addison lived in Central America for less than a year, this period provided the foundation for his life.

He learned the Spanish language and developed a great love for Spanish culture. When Addison later failed the entrance examination for the University of California, his command of Spanish allowed him to attend lectures for a year at the University of Salamanca in Spain. Here his exposure to the unique beauty of Spanish architecture determined the course of his career. After extensive travel in Europe and the Far East, he returned to San Francisco to study architecture as an apprentice to Willis Polk, who later gained fame as the designer of many notable buildings in that city. Mizner es-

tablished his own New York practice in 1904, and during his fourteen years there, his love for Spanish architecture could be seen in the designs of many of his country houses.

Singer purchased the land of a long-time Palm Beach tourist attraction, Joe's Alligator Farm, and decided to build the clubhouse, which he called the Touchstone Convalescents' Club, on Worth Avenue and the shore of Lake Worth. Across the avenue from the main building he planned a series of residential and medical villas. Mizner said that the great beauty of the site made him envision a religious building, "a nunnery, with a chapel built into the lake . . . a mixture built by a nun from Venice, added onto by one from Genoa, with a bit of new Spain of the tropics." When construction began in July 1918 Mizner found that he needed to make his own roof tiles, lighting fixtures, ornamental grills, and furniture, as none of the commercially produced goods satisfied his demanding eye for authenticity. The various little factories established for Singer's club later grew into Mizner Industries, one of the largest manufacturing concerns in West Palm Beach in the 1920s.

By the time the club buildings neared completion, World War I had ended. Although Singer sent thousands of invitations to returning servicemen to come to Palm Beach to convalesce, none were accepted, perhaps because Florida seemed too distant and the veterans wished to remain close to their homes and families. The club never served its original purpose as a convalescing hospital, and in less than a year Singer gave away the expensive hospital equipment he had purchased for the shell-shocked veterans. He also changed its name to the Everglades Club.

The Everglades Club opened on Saturday, January 25, 1919, with twenty-five charter members, and it immediately became the new center of social life in the resort. Singer, who reviewed all applications, assured a membership of the town's wealthiest and most socially prominent citizens. Before the end of the season he announced that membership had reached 300 and had been closed. Even in the first season, before the construction of its tennis courts and golf course, the Everglades became a popular daytime club, probably because, in marked contrast to the hotels, informality prevailed, with Singer leading the way by introducing Riviera-style clothing. Nonetheless, evenings at the Everglades Club remained strictly formal, with costly gowns and elaborate jewelry the rule.

During the first season the club introduced a weekly members' dinner and a daily tea-dance in the orange court. A costume ball, also held during this first season, became one of the club's most popular annual events. Meyer Davis' society orchestra came down from New York to play for the party, and members vied with each other for the most original and elaborate cos-

tume. Singer and many of the other guests often looked to Louis XIV's court for their fancy dress. One writer said that "plain women, with powder and patches . . . became court beauties for an hour." Joseph Riter, a leader of the resort's cultural set and a founder of the organization that became the Society of the Four Arts, once came as a buxom black "mammy," bearing a tray of fruit and vegetables on his head. After the club developed its season of dinners and balls, resorters all but deserted the old hotels.

During the following years Singer asked Mizner to expand the clubhouse several times. Along Worth Avenue he also added a building with shops on the ground floor and apartments for club members above, and a garage and servants' quarters on Peruvian Avenue. Later Singer subdivided some of the club grounds along Golfview Road to allow members to build their own houses. Marion Sims Wyeth, a Princeton graduate and European-trained architect, who came to Palm Beach in 1919 and designed the first Good Samaritan Hospital in West Palm Beach in that year, planned houses along the road for such prominent clients as Jay F. Carlisle, Clarence Geist, and Edward F. Hutton, who at the time was married to Marjorie Merriweather Post.

Edward and Eva Stotesbury had come to Palm Beach every year since their marriage in 1912. "Ned" Stotesbury, a self-made banker and a senior Morgan partner, was one of Philadelphia's wealthiest citizens. Eva, his second wife, had impeccable social credentials. Her father, a Chicago attorney, had been a partner of United States Supreme Court Chief Justice Melville W. Fuller. Her first husband had been a New York and Washington banker and a direct descendant of Oliver Cromwell. Moreover, President William Howard Taft had attended the Stotesburys' wedding in 1912. Nonetheless, neither ever gained complete acceptance by Philadelphia society. Thus Eva Stotesbury directed her considerable talents towards becoming the social leader of Palm Beach. By 1919 her position as "grande dame of the winter set" was recognized by both her fellow resorters and by the all-important society columnists.

Eva Stotesbury decided to assure her leadership of Palm Beach society by building the first great villa since Henry Flagler's Whitehall of nearly two decades earlier. The Stotesburys' Philadelphia architect completed plans for a very large formal Beaux Arts-style mansion for their ocean-to-lake estate just to the north of Wells Road. However, shortly after the opening of the Everglades Club, where Ned Stotesbury was a member of the original board of governors, Mizner saw Eva Stotesbury measuring the club terraces. When he offered to help, she said that the new club made her discontent with the plans for her house. Only a few days later the Stotesburys fired their Philadelphia architect and asked Mizner to prepare new plans for their Palm Beach house.

Mizner designed El Mirasol (the Sunflower) to both accommodate and provide an air of grandeur for Eva Stotesbury's extensive entertaining. As in many of his later oceanfront houses, he located the main rooms on the beach ridge so that they overlooked the sea. In the Stotesbury house he placed the entrance hall on the lower floor, allowing guests a dramatic entry up a broad staircase with low stately risers. Eva, dressed in a gown created by her personal designer and arrayed in a mass of jewels from her vast collection, greeted her guests at the head of the stairs.

The gigantic living room (which one source said could seat 175 people), the dining room of "stately proportions," an open loggia, a long Moorish cloister, and an immense patio allowed Eva to entertain hundreds of guests. Her largest party, the annual celebration of Ned Stotesbury's birthday on February 26, quickly overshadowed the Washington's Birthday Ball, which had been the earlier highlight of the sea-

Eva Stotesbury of Philadelphia was the grande dame of Palm Beach society in the 1920s. Her million-dollar cottage, El Mirasol, and her parties there set the style for the period. Courtesy, HSPBC

son. The guest list grew larger every year with as many as 1,200 people attending by the middle of the 1930s. One source says everyone "from titled personages to the local green-grocer was included. No matter how many people showed up, the buffet table was never empty and the champagne never ran out." Near the end of these parties, and after many glasses of champagne, Ned Stotesbury always played the drums, recalling his Civil War service as a drummer boy, and sang "The Old Family Toothbrush that Hung by the Sink" to the tune of "The Old Oaken Bucket." His guests lustily joined in for the chorus.

Eva Stotesbury entertained regally. While her own staff of butlers and liveried footmen served at small dinner parties, the owner of a local restaurant recalled loaning her sixty extra housemen for one particularly grand occasion. One entire wing of the villa contained guest rooms that remained filled during the season with family and friends. One well-remembered El Mirasol event occurred on Valentine's Day in 1922 when Eva's daughter, Louise Cromwell Brooks, married General Douglas MacArthur. For the service Eva turned the living room into a chapel with an altar before the fireplace and with masses of flowers banked around the room.

El Mirasol, the Stotesburys' grand oceanfront Spanish-Revival mansion, confirmed both Eva's status as society queen and Mizner's status as a fashionable architect. Although several

El Mirasol was the first of Mizner's grand oceanfront estates. Built for Ned and Eva Stotesbury and ready for the season in January 1920, it was their private party palace for the next two decades. In 1923 the segment of North Ocean Boulevard from Wells Road to the Country Club was rerouted to the middle of the island so that the Stotesburys and their neighbors wouldn't have to share the ocean view. Courtesy, HSPBC

mission-style buildings with red-tiled roofs and stucco walls already existed in Palm Beach, including the Beaux Arts Fashion Center and Charles J. Clarke's house, Primavera, these had little in common with the Spanish- and Italian-Revival buildings designed by Mizner. Mizner offered a romantic alternative to the drab architecture of an earlier time. His rambling tile roofs, lofty towers, elegantly detailed yet restrained decoration, sheltered cloisters, richly paneled and beamed rooms, and in particular his flowing floor plans, which opened his rooms to walled patios and broad terraces, created an architecture that seemed completely appropriate for tropical America. When Eva Stotesbury accepted Mizner's architectural vision, other Palm Beach resorters quickly followed.

The new wealth produced by the war allowed growing numbers the luxury of a winter vacation. Their arrival in Palm Beach meant the old hotels began to lose their previous high social standing. The opening of the Everglades Club with its carefully selected membership and the Stotesburys' decision to build a large oceanfront villa together created a new era in the history of the resort. Eva Stotesbury's son, James J.R. Cromwell, invented the term "Palacios Era" to describe how a select few, to retain an air of exclusiveness, now decided to build great mansions in Palm Beach. As these same people usually maintained large houses in Bar Harbor, Newport, or Tuxedo Park, Palm Beach became another stop on their continuing circuit of resort life.

Many of these resorters came to Mizner for the design of their Palm Beach villas. In 1919 he designed houses for Charles and Gurnee Munn and a small villa for himself, which he sold a few months later to Harold S. Vanderbilt. Like El Mirasol all of these were oceanfront houses. In the next five years a Mizner-designed house became a status symbol in the resort. Socially secure scions of the oldest fam-

ilies as well as the newest *nouvelle riche* climbers demanded Mizner's architectural services.

At the same time Mizner also became a social figure in the resort, constantly sought as a guest by society hostesses. A *bon vivant* and *raconteur,* the architect paid for his dinner with amusing stories of the rich, famous, and even royal. Often Mizner made himself the butt of his jokes, telling of his problems as an architect. Soon the legend grew that he often forgot items such as bathrooms, kitchens, or stairways in his houses. Just owning a Mizner-designed house conferred status; owning one in which it was imagined he forgot an essential feature became the ultimate Palm Beach status symbol.

In 1923 alone Mizner had seventeen major projects. While these included substantial villas for society clients like Anthony J. Drexel Biddle, Jr., Arthur D. Clafflin, Angier B. Duke, Edward Shearson, Rodman Wanamaker II, and Henry C. Phipps (two years before Mizner had planned Casa Bendita, an extremely large stone villa for his brother John S. Phipps), the most important project of the year was Playa Riente (Laughing Beach), the oceanfront mansion of Joshua Cosden. Cosden, a streetcar conductor and bank clerk in his native Baltimore, moved to Oklahoma in 1908 and built a $75-million oil empire. In 1919 he married Nell Roeser, sometimes called the most beautiful woman in Oklahoma, and in 1920 his horse John Paul Jones won the Kentucky Derby. The charm, youth, and good looks of both Cosdens soon brought friendships with Mrs. William K. (Birdie) Vanderbilt II, several members of the Phipps family, and other leaders of the new society of the 1920s. They assured their position when they entertained the Prince of Wales during his American visit.

Playa Riente was Mizner's most elaborately decorated and detailed house in Palm Beach. Nell Cosden went to Europe with Mizner to

The aerial view (facing page) shows the extent of the grounds of Playa Riente, with the great square cloister addition on the north and the twenty-five-foot-high seawall. From the magnificent entrance hall (above), inspired by the Valencia stock exchange, there was a tunnel running directly to the beach. The estate, built for Joshua Cosden in 1923, was owned by Anna Thompson Dodge Dillman for thirty years. It was the grandest Mizner mansion in Palm Beach until 1957 when, irritated with high taxes and the town council's refusal to rezone, she had it demolished. Courtesy, HSPBC

purchase furnishings (which included a set of nine gigantic murals depicting the ordeals of Sinbad the Sailor by Spanish artist Jose Maria Sert) and to commission artists to come to

Above: *Hugh Dillman became the second husband of Anna Thompson Dodge after she bought Playa Riente in 1926. During the 1930s he was president of the Everglades Club and an active presence in society. Photo by Kazanjian. Courtesy, HSPBC*

Facing page: *Cielito Lindo, built in 1926 for Jesse Woolworth Donahue, was the first great 1920s mansion to be demolished and subdivided for smaller homesites. Today Kings Road runs through where the living room used to be. However, parts of the original structure remain on both the north and south sides of the road as "complete" houses. Photo by Edward F. Foley. Courtesy, HSPBC*

Palm Beach to help in the decoration of the house.

Mizner placed the great rambling Gothic palace directly on the beach. An arch over the main entrance door contained a bas relief by Percival Dietsch depicting Ponce de Leon's discovery of Florida. (Although an argument raged between supporters of El Mirasol and Playa Riente as to Ponce's landing place in Palm Beach, there is no evidence that he ever landed on the island.) The main door opened directly onto the gigantic stone-floored entrance hall, a room almost sixty feet long and nearly thirty feet high. A massive stone stair-

case, leading to the main reception rooms, filled the entire north end of the hall. The great ballroom where Mizner hung the Sert murals seemed to project out over the beach. The final touches came with the furniture and paintings Nell Cosden purchased in Spain, Florence, and Venice, blended with pieces manufactured by Mizner Industries. Even his critics admitted that Playa Riente proved Mizner's genius as an architect.

The Cosdens enjoyed only two seasons at Playa Riente. A confirmed gambler, the oilman took several worthless fliers on the stock market. Early in 1926 he lost control of his company and was forced to place his various houses, including the one in Palm Beach, on the market. Only a few weeks later Mrs. Horace Elgin Dodge, widow of the automaker, "to avoid the trouble incidental to building such a house as she wanted," purchased Playa Riente for $2,800,000. Hugh Dillman, a former actor and now resort real estate agent and director of the Society of the Arts, a forerunner of the Society of the Four Arts, represented Anna Dodge in the sale. Three weeks later Anna married Dillman at her son's heavily guarded Detroit estate. The sensational press had a field day, pointing to Anna's great wealth and to the fact she was almost twenty years older than her new husband. Although most accounts say the marriage was less than successful, it lasted for twenty-one years. When they divorced in 1947, Anna resumed the Dodge name.

The Dillmans added a 120-feet-square "Gothic Moorish" cloistered patio to Playa Riente, modeled upon an ancient palace of Castilian kings in Toledo, and made it and the large ballroom a center of Palm Beach musical life. Leading figures of the operatic world such as Lily Pons, Gladys Swarthout, Jerome Himes, Lanny Ross, and Claramae Turner sang recitals in the ballroom. After the concerts the Dillmans served champagne suppers in the pa-

Mar-a-Lago on South Ocean Boulevard in Palm Beach was originally built for Marjorie Merriweather Post in the 1920s. Today it is the grandest example of that era remaining in south Florida. Courtesy, HSPBC

tio lighted with tall handmade beeswax candles that cost $100 apiece. One of the most glittering of Playa Riente parties came in April 1941 when the Dillmans entertained the Duke and Duchess of Windsor during their first of many visits to Palm Beach. The 500 guests to the afternoon reception included business and professional people from West Palm Beach as well as the socialites of the resort town.

Two of the last of the great estates of the era arose at the south end of town in the mid-1920s. Cielito Lindo (Taste of Heaven), the $2-million estate of the James Donahues (she was Jesse Woolworth, the dime store heiress), was designed by Marion Sims Wyeth and included the most delicate Moorish detailing of any of the grand houses. Wyeth had also designed Hogarcito, the Edward F. Hutton house on the Everglades Club grounds.

When Mrs. Hutton decided to build a much larger mansion on South Ocean Boulevard, near the Donahue house, she once more asked Wyeth to be her architect. Although Wyeth was responsible for the overall design of the house, before its completion Mrs. Hutton engaged Joseph Urban, the Austrian-trained architect and stage designer, to plan the interior. The house, a sprawling Spanish-Moorish fanta-

sy, surrounded a semicircular cloistered patio with wings for the Huttons, their daughter, guests, and servants radiating from the main building in practically every direction. The gilded and brocaded interior included a dining room modeled from a Roman palazzo with a marble and gold table that reportedly cost a million dollars and seated thirty-six. The Huttons brought house guests to Palm Beach in their private railroad cars and entertained by importing the entire casts of Broadway musicals. By this period Edward Hutton had transformed Marjorie Hutton's Postum holdings into the growing giant of General Foods.

During this period the gulf between the tourists and the "palacios" became even greater as several new and even more exclusive clubs were founded. In the early 1920s everyone swam at The Breakers' beach. In 1926 the Urban-designed Bath and Tennis club opened with a strictly limited membership list. The Gulf Stream Golf Club, fifteen miles south of town, the haven of some of the wealthiest and most social Palm Beachers, had opened two years before. The Mizner-designed clubhouse became the center for the polo complex developed by the Phipps brothers. Finally, to the north of town, Wyeth designed the ultra-exclusive Seminole Golf Club.

The Breakers and the Palm Beach Hotel both were destroyed in a spectacular fire in 1925. The next year a modern fireproof hotel replaced the old wooden Breakers and the huge new Alba Hotel rose on the grounds of the Palm Beach Hotel. After Henry Flagler's death in 1913, Mary Lily closed their Palm Beach house. Her heirs sold the mansion and a twelve-story wing rose on the lakefront to become the Whitehall Hotel. As these new hotels drew even more tourists to the winter resort, the owners of the great mansions withdrew be-

The great spectator event of March 18, 1925, was the burning of the second version of The Breakers, which signaled the end of the era of wooden hotels in southeast Florida. This photograph was taken by Edward F. Foley from the ocean pier just south of the hotel. The third version of The Breakers (above, left) opened the following January. Courtesy, HSPBC

hind their hedges and walls and to the privacy of their exclusive clubs.

By mid-decade Palm Beach had been transformed. The nondescript wooden cottages and hotels of the earlier era had given way to the great Mediterranean-Revival mansions that lined both the ocean and lakefronts. The town called itself the winter Newport and its villas, clubs, hotels, restaurants, and shops all endeavored to maintain this image. One observer said, "Everything about Palm Beach in the 1920s was superlative. Everything was solid gold, extra large, outsized, the most expensive, the most ostentatious, and the most opulent." Certainly Paris Singer had started a revolution.

The peak of the 1925 boom in West Palm Beach looked like this: crowds, cars, and real estate offices. The latter were boosting quick riches for 10 percent down and 100 percent profits within weeks, or even days. Seen here is the Datura Arcade at 201 South Olive Ave. Courtesy, HSPBC

The Land Boom of the 1920s

*H*enry M. Flagler's decision to extend the
Florida East Coast Railway to Biscayne Bay
brought added life to the older communities
south of West Palm Beach and caused the creation of several new towns. These small settlements witnessed a quiet growth during the next
two decades as packing and shipping centers
for the vegetable and fruit producers of the region. Then in the years following World War
I the entire county experienced the frenzy of
rapid development, building, and population increase produced by south Florida's great land
boom of the 1920s.

In 1895 the first settlement south of West
Palm Beach was called Jewell. Although several families lived in the vicinity, Jewell was re-
ally only a post office located in the house of
Samuel and Fannie James, who had homesteaded 186 acres in 1883. After Samuel's
death Fannie sold about 160 acres of her land
to the Palm Beach Farms Company which,
planning a large development, purchased several hundred acres in the area. The company
hired Bryant and Greenwood, a Chicago firm
with salesmen throughout the country, to survey the land, lay out the townsite, and sell the
development. Bryant and Greenwood sold five-
acre farm plots for $250 and gave each pur-
chaser a free lot in the town, which they named
Lucerne.

A random drawing was held in April 1912
to determine the exact location within the development of each buyer's five-acre farm and
town lot. Settlement began immediately, and
by the end of the year there were 308 permanent residents.

When the promoters made application for a
post office, they discovered that another Florida town had claimed the name Lucerne only a
month earlier. The residents of the new town
decided to revive the name Lake Worth, which
had been the name of the first Palm Beach
area post office. In June 1913 the state legislature granted the new city a charter.

The flowering subtropical shrub growing in
profusion in the area gave Lantana its name.
This small settlement near the foot of the lake
served as the northern terminus of the road
that linked lake and bay before the building of
the railroad. In *Early Lantana, Her Neighbors*

Top left: *When it was built in 1912, this concrete-block building at the northeast corner of Federal Highway and Ocean Avenue was the new home of M.B. Lyman's General Store, the main commercial enterprise in Lantana. The two concrete pillars to the right, decorated with oyster shells, formed a gateway for the road to Lantana Point.*

Top right: *Built in 1925, Ye Tower on Federal Highway has been operated by Paul Dunbar ever since. Thus it has the distinction of being the oldest culinary institution in Lantana.*

Bottom: *Looking south at the Boynton station, where crates of produce are ready on the loading dock, one can see the excitement of the once-a-day train stop. The store on Ocean Avenue, to the left of the station, was run for many years by Charles Pierce, the former barefoot mailman. Courtesy, Mary Collar Linehan*

and More Mary Collar Linehan points out that while E.R. Bradley settled there as early as 1877, the Lyman family "deserves the distinction of being the founders of the Town of Lantana." Morris Benson Lyman was born in Canada in 1860. Later his family moved to Michigan, where he received training as a carpenter and boat builder. In 1884 he came to Palm Beach and helped build Dellmoore Cottage for Robert B. Moore, Margretta Pierce's brother.

Lyman's father and other members of the family followed in 1887, and they filed a homestead claim the next year. At that time the Brelsford brothers in Palm Beach still ran the nearest general store. When Lyman heard they wished to sell their schooner, the *Bessie B.*, he purchased it with his earnings as a carpenter and began making regular trips to Jacksonville from the general store and Indian trading post he established on Lantana Point. The name was shortened to Lantana with the granting of a post office in August 1889.

Major Nathan Boynton of Port Huron, Michigan, came to the lake country in 1895 seeking land to develop. He purchased the homestead of Dexter Hubel, and on the beach ridge just south of Lake Worth he built a fifty-room hotel in 1897. More settlers, many from Michigan, began to arrive. They purchased land from Boynton or from the Model Land

This crowd scene in Delray Beach shows what the original bridge over the Intracoastal Waterway looked like around 1910. Courtesy, Delray Beach Historical Society

Company, the real estate arm of the Florida East Coast Railway. This small settlement became Boynton Beach.

In 1894 William S. Linton and his friend David Swinton visited south Florida with plans to establish a new development. The thirty-eight-year-old Linton was then the postmaster of Saginaw, Michigan (he would later be elected to Congress), and Swinton owned a bookstore in the same city. In West Palm Beach they heard of land for sale near the Orange Grove House of Refuge and traveled by barge down the East Coast Canal (later the Intracoastal Waterway) to inspect the junglelike acreage. Although Cecil W. Farrar says in *Incomparable Delray Beach—Its Early Life and Lore* that his Uncle David Swinton did not advise the purchase of the land, Linton paid twenty-five dollars an acre for 160 acres. Moreover, Swinton helped finance the purchase, though Farrar believes it was "to get the trip over" and return to Michigan.

Once back in the North, Linton advertised his development in newspapers in Saginaw, Bay City, and Flint. By the fall of 1895 about ten men had purchased five-acre tracts in the development. In October Linton led them to their new home. The purchasers stayed with the keeper of the House of Refuge until they could clear the land and erect temporary shelters. Once work on the new settlement began, Linton returned to Michigan but as a legacy gave his name to the town.

The pioneers found the work of clearing the land extremely hard. Nonetheless, the rich soil produced bumper crops of tomatoes and green beans. Unfortunately, a freeze during the first year hit as far south as Linton, killing the young plants. Many settlers returned to Michigan. Those who remained received free seeds

75

from Flagler. They also benefited from his extension of the railroad to Miami.

The Florida East Coast Railway brought new settlers, new jobs, and a new lease on life for the citizens of Linton. In 1901, when the population was around 150, the citizens decided to change the name of their town, since they associated Linton with the bad times of the early years. They chose Delray, the name of a Detroit suburb and the former home of one of the early settlers. Ten years later, on September 4, 1911, they incorporated the town of Delray and elected as their first mayor John Shaw Sundy, who had come to south Florida as a superintendent of construction for the railroad.

Boca Raton's first resident, Thomas Moore Rickards, visited the lake country in the winter of 1892. Born in Ohio in 1845, Rickards moved with his family to Missouri, where he received training as a civil engineer and surveyor. At the end of the Reconstruction Era in 1876, Rickards came to central Florida and homesteaded 125 acres at Chandler. He brought his family to Boca Raton after the freeze of the winter of 1894-1895 and built a large two-story house on the east side of the East Coast Canal, just south of today's Palmetto Park Road. At first he acted as land sales representative for the company that dug the canal. (The canal company, like the railroads in Florida, received grants of alternate sections of land along its right-of-way.) With the arrival of the Florida East Coast Railway, Rickards became that company's local agent, surveying, selling land, and even drawing the first general plan for the town. He also planted orange groves for Flagler and James E. Ingraham, railroad vice president in charge of its land operations. Flagler's fifty-five-acre grove commanded the western ridge known as Sunset Hill.

As the railroad's agent Rickards helped establish a Japanese agricultural colony in the town. Jo Sakai, a graduate of New York Un-

iversity's business school, believed that the establishment of Japanese agricultural colonies in America would benefit both lands. The people of his overpopulated country received the opportunity of a new life, while the United States gained the advantage of industrious workers who brought experience in growing tea, rice, and silkworms. The railroad, eager to sell land and to increase freight traffic, encouraged the colony.

The first Japanese arrived in 1904. They called their settlement Yamato, or "large, peaceful country," an ancient name for Japan itself. The Japanese farmers immediately began clearing land and planting vegetables for the winter market. Like their American neighbors they soon switched to pineapples as their cash crop. They were successful in the back-breaking work for several years, and the colony prospered. Then in 1908 a blight hit the pineapple fields of south Florida. By the time the blight had been contained, increased competition from Cuban pineapples made American production unprofitable. Within a few years the Japanese ended their communal experiment. Some of the settlers returned to Japan, while others left to work or settle in other parts of the United States. Those who remained purchased land and returned to raising vegetables for the winter market.

When Rickards moved with his family to the mountains of North Carolina in 1906, George Ashley Long, a Harvard graduate and civil engineer, succeeded him as agent for the railroad. Like Rickards, Long owned extensive land in Boca Raton and cultivated a large citrus grove. Over the years additional settlers came to Boca Raton, but until the 1920s it remained a small settlement of farmers who tended groves or planted fields of winter vegetables.

After World War I the sleepy agricultural character of the county was challenged by the growing interest in development that led to the great Florida land boom of 1924-1925. While

Above: *Jo Sakai, a business school graduate of New York University, established the agricultural colony of Yamato in the scrub pine lands west of the Florida East Coast Railroad. Courtesy, Boca Raton Historical Society*

Left: *George Morikami arrived in the United States in 1906 at the age of twenty to work as a pineapple farmer in the Japanese settlement at Yamato. Nearly seventy years later, as he approached his ninetieth birthday, he gave to the people of Florida 140 acres for a Japanese park and museum. Courtesy, Morikami Museum*

the boom has often been viewed as a Miami phenomenon, no area of the state was immune to the speculation fever. The postwar real estate boom in Palm Beach County began as early as that in Miami, featured schemes that equaled Miami's in their imagination and fantasy, and also captured national attention.

First and foremost among the reasons for the Florida land boom was the mild winter climate that had drawn ever larger numbers of tourists to the state since the days after the Civil War. The increasing use of the automobile and the completion of the network of roads known as the Dixie Highway made Florida easily accessible to the populous cities of the Northeast and Midwest. Prosperity under President Coolidge and the confidence that every American should be rich combined powerfully with stories of great profits made by the earliest investors. Florida encouraged the boom by promising never to pass state income or inheritance taxes.

Driving in south Florida prior to the paving of Dixie Highway in 1917 could be quite a challenge even in dry weather. This picture of U.S. Highway 1, a mile south of Jupiter, was taken in 1916. Courtesy, HSPBC

The first of the large postwar developments sprang up just to the north of West Palm Beach in 1921. It was the brainchild of Harry Seymour Kelsey. A multimillionaire from Massachusetts, Kelsey had made his fortune when, as a young real estate agent, he was stuck with unwanted restaurant equipment. Starting in 1904 with one restaurant in Springfield, Massachusetts, by 1919 his Waldorf chain had outlets in over forty cities.

Kelsey, who had come to Florida to recuperate from pneumonia, saw that the state was ripe for development. He sold his interest in the restaurant chain for over three million dollars and began buying land in the area then known as Silver Beach, the site of his future Kelsey City. By December 1919 he had engaged Olmstead Brothers, the Boston landscape architects and planners, to plat "the perfect city."

The plan called for a complete city including an industrial section well-separated from the areas for houses, businesses, and shopping. The planning firm also designated sites for a civic center, parks, schools, and churches, which Kelsey planned to deed to the city. The entire development was platted and the streets paved

before Kelsey offered a lot for public sale in 1921.

Investor interest in Kelsey City made the development an immediate success. Kelsey built two eighteen-hole golf courses and a town hall and saw two banks chartered and opened in the next four years. In the industrial section Kelsey City Nurseries developed into one of the largest landscapers and growers of landscape plants in the state. Other industries included a brick manufacturer, a decorative stone and tile works, a tire factory, and a lumber mill. A large model dairy also operated in the town.

In 1925 Kelsey sold his Kelsey City and ad-

Harry S. Kelsey, a millionaire restaurant owner from Massachusetts, started the first town-size real estate development of the 1920s in Palm Beach County. Kelsey City, platted and planned by the Bostom firm of Olmstead Brothers, was the earliest sales success in the county. The city name was changed in 1939 to Lake Park. Courtesy, HSPBC

jacent holdings for thirty million dollars to the Royal Palm Beach Company, controlled by a New York banking group and headed by Colonel Henry D. Lindsley, the former mayor of Dallas. Before the company could complete plans for development, the Florida land boom ended and with it the market for Kelsey City real estate.

Just before the bust, Kelsey and Paris Singer built the Palm Beach Winter Club, which included a clubhouse and golf course. Later Sir Harry Oakes assumed management and planned to make it the center for a "posh" country club development. In 1939 the Florida legislature, at the request of the Kelsey City Garden Club, changed the name of the town to Lake Park. Kelsey, who lost his fortune in the bust, refused to give up. At the time of his death in 1957 he was promoting Utopia, a retirement village he planned to build west of Miami.

The early success of Kelsey City encouraged local business and real estate boosters to promote the county. Various campaigns were designed to bring in visitors. One project called for local residents to mail 100,000 postcards before the 1924-1925 winter season bearing "pictures and messages calculated to draw friends and relatives to the Palm Beaches." The West Palm Beach Chamber of Commerce published 50,000 publicity booklets, featuring the "best-appearing young men and women" in the area to show the "allurements of this section," and asked county businessmen to join the All-Florida Development Conference in raising $60,000 to advertise the state "throughout the world."

Once the tourists arrived in Palm Beach County, the goal was to sell them land. To accomplish this a continuing flow of stories in the *Palm Beach Post* and the newly established evening newspaper, the *Palm Beach Times,* told of the opening of new projects, developments, and subdivisions; of the great profits made from land and real estate sales; of the rising values in building activities and bank clearings; of famous individuals purchasing land in the area; and of the projects for community improvements. Boosters marshaled these stories to show Palm Beach County as a dynamic and fast-growing area in which people already had confidence, an area where real estate investments could only increase in value.

Since a land boom, like a stockmarket boom, is based on confidence that today's purchase will be worth more tomorrow and even more the next day, profits were particularly emphasized. The newspaper stories told of property reselling several times in just a few weeks and its price doubling at each sale. West Palm Beach real estate increased in value $750 an hour when a buyer paid $11,000 for a 100-foot lot on Dixie Highway at three in the afternoon and resold it at five for $12,500. In Palm Beach a thirty-two acre tract purchased in 1916 for $75,000 from a homesteader sold in 1925 for a million. Nine months later the same tract, subdivided into building lots, sold at auction for $1,757,647.

Business leaders also emphasized the "destiny" of West Palm Beach to become the largest city on the southeast Florida coast, surpassing even Miami in population. They claimed every advantage of the other cities, such as climate, waterways, and natural beauty, and added to these the great wealth of the new farming industry in the Everglades and the plans to make West Palm Beach the terminus of both a cross-state highway and a new railroad.

The height of the land boom in Palm Beach County came, as in all of Florida, in the winter season of 1924-1925 and lasted into the following autumn months. Hardly a week passed without the announcement of the creation of a new development or the founding of a new city. Some typical promotions described small subdivisions in suburban West Palm Beach, such as the thirty-four-lot tract in Santa Lucia "grabbed up by investors" between nine and four on the first day of sales. Others embraced hundreds of acres: a West Palm Beach firm laid out a 525-acre "smaller Coral Gables" with a Venetian theme that utilized the lakes of western Boynton Beach.

One of the earliest large projects came in February 1925 when Paris Singer joined with Kelsey to develop a great resort city on the is-

Above: *This 1947 aerial of Hypoluxo Island shows the southern end of Lake Worth with the Intracoastal Waterway continuing on to Boynton and Delray.*

Right: *Madame Louis Jacques Balsan, the former Consuelo Vanderbilt, and former Duchess of Marlborough by her first marriage, bought the Hannibal D. Pierce homestead on the southern part of Hypoluxo Island in 1929. Photo by Van Durand. Courtesy, HSPBC*

land to the north of Palm Beach. In fact, Singer requested permission to join his new resort to the old by an aerial ferry across the inlet. Newspaper reports said that Singer's backers included Edward F. Hutton, Anthony J. Drexel Biddle, Jr., Gurnee and Charles Munn, and John S. Pillsbury. Their plan to spend three million dollars in immediate improvements on the island included a large hotel.

A Boca Raton project captured the most attention of all and became in many ways the archetypal boomtime development. The creation of Palm Beach architect Addison Mizner, the Boca Raton project's tremendous size, presumed social cachet, and bluechip financial backing placed it immediately in the forefront of Florida land schemes.

Mizner announced on April 15, 1925, that he planned to build a $6-million hotel called the Castillo del Rey on the beach at Boca Raton to spearhead his great 16,000-acre development. The modern fireproof 1,000-room hotel would be built with the backing of a syndicate that included leaders of the American financial, social, and entertainment worlds, such as Harold Vanderbilt and his brother William K. Vanderbilt II, Paris Singer, Rodman Wanamaker, T. Coleman du Pont, Clarence H. Geist, Irving Berlin, Madame Frances Alda, and Elizabeth Arden.

By the time the Mizner company accepted its first "reservation" for the purchase of land on May 14, its publicity proclaimed that the stockholders represented "considerably over one-third of the entire wealth of the United States." The first offering of lots was sold in both Miami and West Palm Beach. In the latter city, automobiles jammed the streets for blocks, and "pandemonium reigned in the office" as an opening-day record of $2,100,000 in lot sales was established.

When the Ritz-Carlton organization took over the projected beachfront hotel, Mizner announced plans to begin immediately on construction of a 100-room inn on Lake Boca Raton. Other development proposals for the town included a 160-foot-wide road called Camino Real, a casino, an air terminal, a deepened inlet and yacht basin, a Venetian lake with gondolas, a Spanish village, and Irving Berlin's Cabaret with the best theatrical talent of the world. A second offering of lots in late May again saw over two million dollars in sales.

As the Mizner interests continued their sales pitch, other developers, anxious to cash in on the great Palm Beach County venture, joined

them in Boca Raton. In early June George W. Harvey, a West Palm Beach and Boston real estate man, announced the development of Villa Rica at Boca Raton, a complete 1,400-acre modern city. Harvey proposed to spend two million dollars immediately on a Florida East Coast Railway station and on the 100-room Villa Rica Inn, both designed in the prevailing Spanish style.

By September the new south county developments included Del-Raton Park (to the north of Villa Rica), Boca del Faro (to the south on the Broward County line), and Del Boca (to the west and north). As activity picked up in the fall W.A. Mathes, a West Palm Beach businessman, purchased a tract to the east of Del-Raton for three million dollars to develop an American Venice. G. Frank Croissant, a Chicago developer who had just sold all of Croissant Park in Fort Lauderdale, announced Croissantania, a 2,360-acre tract north of the Mizner land and west of the Dixie Highway at prices "available to workingmen who could aid in the upbuilding of the entire community." Soon after came Boca Raton Heights, located south of Palmetto Park Road; Boca Vista, on the highlands of Boca Raton, thirty feet above sea level and "overlooking the entire city"; and Boca Centrale, "in the heart of the city."

By fall the Mizner organization had sold over eleven million dollars' worth of lots and acreage. However, this money did not come in all at once, since the typical buyer only made a down payment of 20 to 25 percent in the first year. Meanwhile, the Mizner organization had payments of its own to make for its land purchases and for the many expensive projects be-

Actress Marie Dressler and film star Richard Barthelmiess (right) were friends of Addison Mizner, who invited them to the grand opening of his Ritz-Carlton Cloister Inn in Boca Raton in January 1926. Courtesy, HSPBC

gun in the town. It needed a continuing high volume of sales to meet these obligations. Unfortunately, in late August purchases of Boca Raton land slowed, in part because of northern attacks on dishonest Florida real estate claims. To stimulate sales, the company pledged to stand by its advertised promises, adding this line to its newspaper publicity: "Attach this advertisement to your contract for deed, it becomes a part thereof."

Problems for Florida's development had surfaced during the summer. A breakdown in transportation services proved to be one of the most serious, since the southeast coast was dependent upon supplies from outside the state to continue the gigantic building programs. Because of massive freight car congestion (hundreds of loaded cars remained in south Florida railroad yards), the Florida East Coast Railway embargoed all but perishable goods in August 1925. The embargo soon spread to railroads in other parts of the state and brought most construction to a halt.

In October the boom all but ended for the Mizner Development Corporation and Boca Raton. T. Coleman du Pont, the chairman of the company's board of directors, resigned along with several other members. They objected to the use of their names in company advertising, claiming the ads implied that they personally guaranteed the millions of dollars' worth of construction planned for the city. They also objected to attaching promotional advertisements to deeds.

Only a week before resigning from the board du Pont had hosted at his Waldorf-Astoria Hotel in New York a "Truth About Florida" seminar to try to counteract the unfavorable publicity. A delegation headed by Governor John W. Martin attempted to convince northern newspaper and magazine reporters that the great increase in property values in the state represented real worth. The meeting may, in fact, have alerted du Pont and several of his

associates to the growing problems in the Florida real estate market. Unfortunately for Boca Raton, they decided to announce their resignation from the Mizner board in a letter to the *New York Times.* This letter marked the beginning of the end for the Mizner Development Corporation and probably also for the Florida land boom.

Du Pont, who with his cousins Alfred and Pierre incorporated the family powder firm into the gigantic E.I. duPont deNemours Company in 1902, had brought financial stability to the Mizner organization. His decision to quit the board was seen as a warning to prospective buyers. His letter to the *New York Times* further weakened the small investor's confidence. As one writer said, it "put a wet blanket on the entire boom." Land sales and building permits in Florida overall reached a high point in October 1925. Although there was no abrupt end to land sales, after this month it was all downhill.

The Boca Raton development struggled on as a few early projects neared completion. December saw the opening of the Administration Building at Camino Real and Dixie Highway and announcements of even more buildings to come, including a new town hall. On Christmas Eve Mizner entertained some of his former Palm Beach clients at his new lakeside inn, now renamed the Ritz-Carlton Cloister. The formal opening of the hotel came on February 6, 1926, with another society dinner hosted by the architect. Footmen wearing red coats with gold braid served a "Lucullan repast" to 500 guests.

By spring, almost everyone knew the Florida land boom had ended. The purchasers of the first lots sold in the early spring of 1925 now found their second installments due. Large numbers of these investors had bought for speculation alone, planning to sell for a large profit in less than a year. After du Pont's resignation these speculators found it impossible to make a profit on their lots. In fact, they found no buyers at all. Many could not afford the second payment; others, seeing the declining prices, "refused to send good money after bad." Almost all Florida developers faced the same situation. Some, like Mizner, committed themselves to huge expenditures for improvements, confident of a continuous flow of money from new sales and yearly payments on previous sales. When the flow of money stopped, they were unable to meet their commitments, and most ended in bankruptcy.

By the fall of 1926 Mizner yielded the management of the development to a Chicago corporation headed by the brother of United States Vice President Charles Dawes. The continuing failure to sell land and a hurricane in September 1926 convinced Dawes that there was no hope for the development. After struggling through another season, in May 1927 the Mizner corporation went into involuntary bankruptcy. Ultimately, Clarence Geist, one of the original backers, purchased the remaining assets of the company and reopened the hotel as the private Boca Raton Club.

The Ritz-Carlton Cloister Inn—conceived, designed, and built in the heat of the Florida land boom—opened in February 1926, just as real estate speculation was cooling off. Courtesy, Donald W. Curl

The Farmers Central Bank on Clematis Street at Olive
Avenue failed in 1926, as it ran out of cash to pay doubt-
ing depositors. Its mortgage loans on overvalued Florida
real estate recovered perhaps five cents on the dollar.
In 1926, Florida led the nation in bank failures and
defaulted mortgages. Courtesy, HSPBC

The Land Bust and the Depression

n 1920 only 8,659 people lived in West lm Beach. A boy living on Jessamine Street the edge of downtown in that year recalled ding the family cow only a few blocks west pasture. Before the end of the land boom little country town became a city. The 30 census recorded 26,610 residents, and haps as many as 30,000 lived in the city ring the last year of the boom. Although a came only to take advantage of the boom-e opportunities and left with the bust, most yed.

Moreover, by the end of the boom West lm Beach looked like a city. During the mid-years of the twenties a massive construction gram brought dozens of new buildings to its wntown. Many of the largest buildings were signed by the architectural firm of Harvey d Clarke. Henry Stephen Harvey, a native of ississippi, met L. Phillips Clarke at the Uni-rsity of Pennsylvania architectural school. ey later formed a Philadelphia firm and in 21 decided to open a West Palm Beach of-e. Clarke was the grandson of Palm Beach oneer Charles J. Clarke. During the next five

years the firm designed dozens of buildings on both sides of the lake, including the new town hall and fire station, Gus' Bath, the Palm Beach Stores, Inc., the Murray Building, and several large houses in Palm Beach.

In West Palm Beach their Dixie Court and New Pennsylvania hotels and million-dollar Guaranty, ten-story Comeau, and ornate Alfred H. Wagg Corporation buildings created a city skyline that remained virtually unaltered until the flurry of construction during the 1980s. The firm counted among its smaller commissions Holy Trinity Episcopal Church, the Palm Beach County Library, the First American National Bank and Trust Company, the Palm Beach Post, apartments, and several arcade buildings. While involved in the physical transformation of downtown West Palm Beach, Harvey also ran a successful campaign to become mayor of the city in 1924.

The tallest "skyscraper" constructed in West Palm Beach in the 1920s was the only major building not designed by Harvey and Clarke. Paradoxically, it was known as the Harvey Building, for its owner George W. Harvey, the

Boston developer and promoter of Villa Rica in Boca Raton.

Further evidence of West Palm Beach's city status came in 1926 when the telephone company announced it had 1,500 business subscribers and prepared to issue its first directory with yellow pages. Southern Bell had taken over the local company several years earlier. As part of a million-dollar improvement program for the greater Palm Beach area it built a four-story building on Fern Street and installed equipment to convert all area telephones to the dial system.

As the 1920s land boom subsided, West Palm Beach took steps to become a seaport. The inlet never had sufficient width or depth to allow major oceangoing vessels to enter the lake. Earlier attempts at dredging had proved meaningless as the first "nor'easter" always clogged the cut. In 1926 General George W. Goethals, the engineer of Panama Canal fame, agreed to deepen and widen the inlet and construct a twenty-four-foot channel to a harbor on the mainland. His plan included the construction of jetties to prevent sand closing the channel. The *Mary Weems* opened the port as its first passenger vessel on January 3, 1927.

The boom period also saw West Palm Beach become the terminus of two major cross-state transportation arteries. In January 1925 the Seaboard Air Line Railroad began regular train service from the city. The Seaboard had long operated in northern and western Florida. S. Davies Warfield, the line's president (and

Facing page, top: *The skyline of West Palm Beach, a result of the 1920s boom, was essentially unchanged for half a century until the surge of 1970s construction. Courtesy, HSPBC*

Facing page, bottom: *The county courthouse was built in 1916 on Dixie Highway north of Second Street in West Palm Beach. The building pictured here is still standing on the same site but has been completely covered up by the additions of the last twenty years. Courtesy, HSPBC*

uncle of Wallis Warfield, who often visited the county after she became the Duchess of Windsor), decided to challenge the Florida East Coast Railway's hold on the southeast coast. After purchasing extensive central Florida land and the right-of-way into West Palm Beach, he saw the new line of 204 miles completed during the summer and fall of 1924 as over 6,000 men worked day and night laying two to three miles of track every twenty-four hours. Beginning at Coleman, on the Seaboard's main line to Tampa, the new route ran in a nearly straight line from the center of the state to the coast, cutting travel time between West Palm Beach and Tampa from eighteen to seven hours.

Originally Warfield planned to make West Palm Beach the terminus of the road. When the line's immediate success doubled the price of the bonds sold to finance the extension, he financed a new $25-million bond issue. With the additional money he extended the Seaboard all the way to Naples on the west coast and south to Miami on the east coast in 1927. Although West Palm Beach business interests regretted the decision to extend the line, having the second railroad during the very height of the boom certainly benefited the city. Moreover, the firm of Harvey and Clarke received the commission to design the $50,000 Spanish-Revival Seaboard station in West Palm Beach as well as twenty-one other depots along the railroad's lines on both Florida coasts.

The second cross-state artery quickly became more important for local interests as it brought closer ties between the coastal and western sections of Palm Beach County. The Conners Highway officially opened on July 4, 1924, as a toll road owned by William J. "Fingy" Conners. Conners received his nickname after he broke a finger in a fight on the Buffalo, New York, docks while making his multimillion-dollar fortune. He vacationed at the Royal Poinciana Hotel as early as 1902 and may have served as cartoonist George McManus'

With the opening of the Conners Highway on July 4, 1924, automobiles had direct access from the east coast to Lake Okeechobee, with connecting links on to Tampa. This made possible a round trip from the lake to the county seat in one day. Courtesy, HSPBC

model for Jiggs in the comic strip "Bringing Up Father." Conners began buying land on Lake Okeechobee in 1917 and eventually acquired more than 12,000 acres, including the unsold town site of Okeechobee City. In order to attract buyers he approached the state legislature in 1923 for permission to build the first road from the east coast to the lake. His road ran nineteen miles along the West Palm Beach Canal from Twenty Mile Bend to the lake and then thirty-three miles along the lakeshore to Okeechobee City. There the highway connected with other state roads leading to Tampa, giving the lower portion of Florida its first cross-state route.

Conners invited everyone to join a motorcade over the new highway on the morning of the Fourth of July for a "great celebration" at Okeechobee City. Governor Cary A. Hardee praised Conners' accomplishment before a crowd of 15,000, which then enjoyed the plentiful barbecue of the cattle country and paid their toll for traveling on the new road, even on that first day. After Conners' death West Palm Beach acquired the highway in 1929. Later the State Road Department took it over when the city defaulted on its purchase bonds.

Before Conners built his highway, the only direct route between the coastal and western sections of the county was the West Palm Beach Canal, opened in 1917. A boat carrying mail, passengers, and freight left West Palm Beach early every Monday, Wednesday, and Friday morning for the all-day trip up the canal to the lake. The canal was a product of Governor Napoleon Bonaparte Broward's championing of Everglades drainage. He had convinced the state legislature to pass a comprehensive drainage law in 1905 to reclaim swamp and overflow lands. The state action produced a minor boom in Everglades land sales.

In 1908 Richard J. Bolles, a real estate promoter with interests throughout the nation,

The Bolles Hotel, seen here just after opening in April 1912, was built at Lake Harbor on Lake Okeechobee to accommodate prospective land buyers. There was a demonstration farm nearby to show that crops could indeed grow in the rich muck of the area. Photo by F.W. Hunt. Courtesy, Historical Association of South Florida

purchased 108,000 acres on the south shore of Lake Okeechobee. At this time the funds for drainage operations gave out. To continue the program, Broward persuaded Bolles to purchase an additional 500,000 acres from the state for a million dollars. Florida pledged to use Bolles' payments, which extended over an eight-year period, to continue to drain and survey the land. Bolles then formed a number of development companies and employed a staff of glib salesmen who toured the rural communities of the Midwest selling Everglades farms.

In 1912 the promoter built the Bolles Hotel and started a demonstration farm. Prospective customers came by steamboat (up the Caloosahatchee River from Fort Myers, and later up the New River Canal from Fort Lauderdale) to the hotel, described as "somewhat luxuriously equipped for a jungle structure."

Unfortunately, Bolles' organization sold land faster than the state could drain it. In fact, in *Lake Okeechobee*, Alfred and Kathryn Hanna titled their chapter on Bolles and the other ear-

ly developers "Land by the Gallon." A Washington newspaper of the time called Bolles' sale of Everglades farms "one of the biggest land swindles in history." Angry purchasers brought numerous suits. During one trial an attorney asked a witness how she felt about coming to Florida and discovering her land covered with water. Much to the amusement of the jury she answered, "I was entirely at sea." Bolles survived continuing efforts to prosecute him for fraud because he honestly believed in the worth of his Everglades properties.

State efforts to reclaim Everglades land continued with the digging of the St. Lucie River

and West Palm Beach canals. As usable farm land became a reality, settlers moved to the western portion of the county. Before 1920 pioneer settlements existed at what later became Pahokee (Seminole for "grassy waters"), Lake Harbor (site of the Bolles Hotel), Belle Glade (first known as Hillsborough Canal), Okeelanta (named for its location between Lake Okeechobee and the Atlantic Ocean), Bacom Point (named for its first settler), and Sand Cut.

In 1921 the United States Department of Agriculture established a breeding station for sugar cane at Canal Point, and the University of Florida placed an agricultural experiment station at Belle Glade in 1923. Farmers learned that they could produce good crops on the rich muck near the lake's shore. Unfortunately, most of the drained land consisted of saw-grass peat and was less productive. Researchers at the experiment station soon found that adding small amounts of copper and manganese made the reclaimed land highly productive, too.

Everglades drainage and settlement took place during years of low rainfall and no severe tropical storms. In 1922 and 1924 heavy rains raised the level of the lake and caused extensive flooding, though no lives were lost. Governor John W. Martin dedicated his administration to continuing the drainage project as an answer to the flooding. Then, after a very dry winter

Facing page, top: *This 1910 picture shows the dredging of the West Palm Beach Canal to Lake Okeechobee. Courtesy, HSPBC*

Facing page, bottom: *The winter vegetable crops produced along Lake Okeechobee became a large-scale modern agricultural enterprise in the years preceding the Second World War. Courtesy, Belle Glade Historical Society*

Above, right: *The eye of the 1928 hurricane passed through Lantana and on to West Palm Beach. Flooding around Lake Okeechobee caused hundreds of deaths, which led to the construction of a dike system during the 1930s. Courtesy, HSPBC*

and spring in 1926, summer rains raised the lake level to a new high. That September, the Labor Day hurricane that devastated Miami moved northwestward across the Everglades and deposited the floodwaters of the lake onto tiny Moore Haven in Hendry County. More than 300 people were killed and the town was leveled.

Although damage from the storm had been minimal in Palm Beach County, those living on the eastern and southern shores of the lake demanded that the drainage projects continue. When Governor Martin convinced the state legislature to authorize additional bonds, he faced opposition from landowners who wanted their taxes adjusted according to benefits received from drainage. Challenges to the bond sales kept the issue in court for over a year.

The securities were still unsold when on September 16, 1928, a powerful hurricane struck Palm Beach and moved westward across West Palm Beach to the lake, destroying Belle Glade. A weakened eight-foot dike at the south end of the lake collapsed, raising floodwaters from four to eight feet in an hour. The devastation extended from Port Mayaca on the north to Lake Harbor near the western county border.

Although it was estimated that over 2,000 people died in the storm, the actual number will never be known. Many bodies were never recovered, washed into the Everglades by powerful floodwaters, and many victims were transient Bahamian agricultural workers who were never reported missing. The physical damage was also great. From Palm Beach to the lake the storm knocked buildings off their foundations, flattened houses, and swept the landscape.

The end of the land boom had already weakened Florida's ability to finance additional flood controls, even if state leaders could gain support for their plans. South Florida was still suffering the devastation of the 1928 hurricane when the stock market collapsed in October 1929. Doyle E. Carlton, who succeeded Martin as governor in January 1929, realized that the state could not finance a solution for the problems of the reclaimed lands. He sought aid from the federal government.

The Rivers and Harbors Act of 1930 authorized the secretary of war to provide deeper and wider channels for the Caloosahatchee and St. Lucie rivers and to construct a new thirty-one-foot dike around the southern end of the lake. In 1935 the Army Corps of Engineers took over the ongoing project. Since then over half a billion dollars have been spent to maintain and improve the project. As Charlton W. Tebeau observed in *A History of Florida,* "there is not yet any real assurance that plans for water control are at all adequate." Fortunately, no major hurricane has yet put the project to the test.

Even before the 1926 hurricane and the economic troubles that came in its wake, the Palm Beach County business community recognized that hard times lay ahead. The problems of the Mizner Development Corporation, which pricked the bubble of prosperity, were widespread. Speculators had pushed prices so high that they could no longer find buyers. Development after development failed, and their failure caused real estate businesses, architectural offices, construction firms, building-supply companies, banks, and even the towns and cities of the county to face ruin. As early as June 1926 three West Palm Beach banks with thousands of depositors failed. One of these was the Commercial Bank and Trust Company, whose largest depositor, with a $700,000 account, was the City of West Palm Beach.

The spectacular growth of the boom period forced the county's municipalities to expand services. They constructed new water purification and sewage treatment plants, built seawalls, laid out and paved streets, acquired park lands and public beaches, and erected bathing pavilions and recreational facilities. In many cases the growing population also demanded more public servants and new town and city halls to house them. Bonds issued by the municipalities paid for all of these improvements. The government leaders saw the new skyscrapers, hotels, stores, and houses, the new subdivisions and developments, and assumed the money to pay off the bonds would come from an ever-increasing tax base.

When the banks failed—and from Boca Raton to Jupiter most did—depositors lost their savings. When businesses failed, their employees lost their jobs. When the developments failed, governments lost their tax base to make bond payments. West Palm Beach's fund to maintain its cemetery emptied. The American-LaFrance Company attempted to foreclose on Boca Raton's fire engine. All but basic municipal services ended everywhere. Most cities had no money for principal payments on their bonds; many found it necessary to postpone interest payments. West Palm Beach refunded its bonds in 1936 when the bonded debt stood at

Seldom-photographed Clarence H. Geist, seen here with his wife, became a figure of almost monarchal influence in Boca Raton after buying out the bankrupt Mizner Development Corporation. Courtesy, Boca Raton Historical Society

Developing the Boca Raton Club as his private domain, Geist more than doubled the size of Mizner's hotel buildings. Courtesy, Donald W. Curl

twenty million dollars and the assessed property valuation at only eighteen million. The city refunded again in 1939 and 1944 and only made the final debt payment in 1951. Almost every town and city in the county felt the economic depression at least two years before the crash of the New York stock market.

As the rest of the county suffered the hardship of depression, two of its towns continued to prosper. Both Palm Beach and Boca Raton quickly overcame the problems of the bust. In 1928 Clarence H. Geist purchased the Mizner Development Corporation property for $71,000 in a bankruptcy sale and turned the small hotel into the exclusive Boca Raton Club.

Geist, one of Mizner's original backers in the Boca Raton venture, made his fortune in utilities. He owned so many water companies that one author says his nickname became "the water boy." By the time he purchased the Boca Raton property, estimates of his fortune ran as high as fifty million dollars. Legend holds that he was blackballed by the Everglades Club, so in retaliation he purchased Mizner's hotel to make it an even more exclusive club. However, the story is apocryphal. Although Geist seems to have been an uninhibited eccentric, who perhaps appeared coarse to Palm Beach's polite society, this did not keep him from membership in the Everglades Club. In fact, his Palm Beach house was on Golf View Road on the club grounds. As for the origin of his plans to establish the Boca Raton Club, several years before he purchased the Mizner properties Geist remarked to a reporter that he planned to build a winter club in Florida. He already owned a summer club in New Jersey.

The Cloister Inn contained only 100 guest rooms. Geist immediately began an $8-million building program to increase the hotel's size to 450 rooms. The New York architectural firm of Schultze and Weaver, who had just completed the Waldorf-Astoria in that city and The Breakers in Palm Beach, designed the additions to Mizner's small inn. The improvements also included new indoor and outdoor swimming pools, the lofty cathedral dining room, a second golf course, and a cabana club with a third swimming pool on the beach.

The club opened for the 1929 season, though the improvements continued for several years. Geist required club members to purchase $5,000 in stock in the Spanish River Land Company, the development wing of his Boca Raton operations, but he charged only modest dues of $100 annually.

Without question Geist ruled his club with an iron hand. His eccentricities became legend: movies began only when he arrived, he walked through the elaborately decorated lobby in his bathrobe, and his chauffer-driven car often followed him across the golf links.

His presence was also felt in the town. As the largest property holder and the employer of many of its citizens, Geist believed he could run Boca Raton like a fiefdom. He had the date of town elections changed from the fall to February so that he and the many seasonal employees of the club could vote, giving him almost complete control of the government. Boca Raton officials routinely asked his approval before making major decisions. Moreover, his arrival each season brought the town's entire population and the club band to the railroad station to officially greet him.

Good looks, talent, and a cultured European background made Maurice Fatio an extremely successful young architect in Palm Beach society. His firm seemed to thrive despite the hard times of the Florida bust and the stock-market crash. Courtesy, HSPBC

The club never made a profit. In fact, its attention to detail, excellent kitchen, and its owner's absolute insistence on privacy cost many thousands of dollars each year. But cost was of no apparent concern to Geist, and when he died in 1938, he left the club $100,000 a year for the next five years.

Palm Beach society never knew of the real estate bust. While James H.R. Cromwell's Fort Lauderdale development ended in foreclosure with the land returned to the original owners, his mother and stepfather, the Edward Stotesburys, continued to live in the grand tradition. The novelist Joseph Hergesheimer, visiting the resort in 1930, said El Mirasol "was, perhaps, the last place I know of in the United States where the grand manner was still at a formal perfection. Nowhere else, I was certain, were there so many and such unobtrusive servants. The scale of everything was spacious." The writer realized that El Mirasol's day had passed, even in Palm Beach: "When this house was gone, when its exact courtesy was lost, none would ever take its place."

Although Mizner's great houses continued to be admired, he never reestablished his Palm Beach practice after the debacle of Boca Raton. The largest houses of the late 1920s and early 1930s were designed by the young, talented, and very social Maurice Fatio, a Swiss-born and -trained architect who headed the Florida office of Treanor and Fatio. In these years Fatio designed large villas for Colonel and Mrs. Jacques Balsan (the former Consuelo Vanderbilt and Duchess of Marlborough) and for her brother Harold S. Vanderbilt in Manalapan, as well as for Otto Kahn, Joseph E. Widner, Mortimer Schiff, and William J. McAneeny in Palm Beach. In this period many of Fatio's houses showed the definite inspiration of the Tuscan villa, though he designed a French-Norman lakefront house in 1928 for his future mother-in-law, Mrs. Charles C. Chase.

As the 1930s advanced, the great Spanish palaces of the previous decade gave way to smaller and less formal houses, often in Georgian, Bermudian, British or French West Indies Colonial, and Monterey styles. Howard Major, leaving a Long Island country-house practice to join Mizner's firm in 1925, called for British Colonial styles in Palm Beach, arguing that they were more suited to the tropical climate and American heritage than the popular Spanish and Italian villas. To prove his point he built six small Bermuda-style townhouses on Peruvian Avenue. Although these "Major Alley" houses found many admirers, at that time Palm Beach still decreed Spanish architecture. When John L. Volk, who also came to Florida from New York in the mid-1920s, designed a British West Indies Colonial house on the lakefront in 1932 and built his own house in the Bermuda style three years later, the time was right for the change.

These new architectural styles marked a change in Palm Beach society caused by the depression. Although most regular resorters suffered little from the stock market crash, incidents like the Veterans' Bonus March, the calls for national economic reforms, the New Deal programs of the Roosevelt administration, and especially the increase in income taxes convinced many that flaunting one's wealth was no longer good policy. As Fortune pointed out in 1936, "Life in Palm Beach is above all else private: there is little venturing into public places. You entertain in your own home or you tour among the homes of your friends. High walls shelter you from the grim world of the anonymous poor." The season gradually expanded in the 1930s to six months and more. The new houses were designed to be lived in rather than to be theatrical settings for the entertainments of a short and extravagant season.

The fashionable resort hotels, which had once thrived on the annual visits of the well-to-do, were in a state of decline by the 1930s. The Royal Poinciana had become antiquated,

The first public junior college in the state of Florida was founded in 1933 in this building on Gardenia Street in West Palm Beach. It grew out of the Palm Beach County High School, with which it shared facilities and faculty for fifteen years. Its founding required a brave effort during the depression. Today with four campuses and over 13,000 full-time students, it has become a major educational enterpise. Courtesy, HSPBC

sometimes referred to as a "Victorian relic." When the Kenan family inherited the Flagler hotels on the death of Mary Lily Kenan Flagler in 1917, they decided that the expense of maintaining and modernizing the old wooden hotel and its diminishing clientele no longer justified its operation. In 1935 an era in Palm Beach's history ended when the Royal Poinciana was torn down. Many builders bought the lumber, still sound after forty years, and used it in houses throughout the county. John Volk purchased many items from the hotel and used the lovely columns from the main portico for a house in Hypoluxo. After 1935 all that remained of the Palm Beach landmark was a former lath house and a number of royal poinciana trees. One writer mentioned that for

years these trees, although completely uncared for, bloomed every spring, "as if in memory" of the old hotel.

During the depression years Palm Beach County gained several of the educational and cultural institutions that continue to enrich its life. In 1933 the county school board approved the establishment of Florida's first junior college. Howell Lee Watkins, the principal of

The Society of the Four Arts Library was designed by local architect Maurice Fatio and opened in January 1938. The attractively laid out gardens to the south and east represent a long-term commitment by the Garden Club. Photo by Frank Turgeon, Jr. Courtesy, HSPBC

Palm Beach High School, realized that many of his graduating seniors could find no jobs in that depression year. In order to give these students hope for the future he persuaded Joseph Youngblood, superintendent of county schools, to join him in a campaign to establish Palm Beach Junior College. The two men spoke to groups across the county and gained the support of service clubs, which named representatives to a college advisory board. Seven high school teachers with master's degrees volunteered to teach the college courses without pay. Youngblood assumed the presidency of the new institution and Watkins became the unpaid dean.

During its first years the college offered no formal degree program. Nonetheless, the University of Florida and Florida State College for Women helped develop a curriculum that allowed transfers to the senior institutions. Many other Florida schools also accepted the work completed at Palm Beach Junior College. In 1939 the school received its first public funds and began the process for accreditation, which it gained from the Southern Association of Colleges and Schools in 1942.

Since the early 1920s the Society of Arts, under the direction of Joseph Riter and later Hugh Dillman, sponsored musical programs such as the 1927 concert of the Cleveland Symphony Orchestra in the newly opened Paramount Theatre and art shows in the Whitehall Hotel, the former Flagler mansion. The society received informal support from Riter, who opened the music room in his lakefront house for recitals, and from the Stotesburys, Henry Seligman, Paris Singer, and other society leaders of the resort.

In 1934 a group of the town's citizens, spearheaded by Maud Howe Elliot, decided to organize a society to promote interest in art, literature, music, and science, and ultimately to found a library and art museum. The Society of the Four Arts received its charter in February 1936. In that same year Colonel Edward R. Bradley provided a large vacant store in the Spanish Provincial Building (now the Embassy Apartments) on Royal Palm Way, where the society held its first show of over fifty old-master paintings borrowed largely from Palm Beach collectors. The show included Rembrandt's "Aristotle Contemplating the Bust of Homer," lent by gallery owner Sir Joseph Duveen. Twenty-five years later the Metropolitan Museum purchased the painting for $2,300,000 at auction.

In 1937 the society bought land just north of its temporary home from the Phipps interests. For the society's new building Maurice Fatio, an original member of its board of trustees, donated his architectural services. The society moved into the Italian-style structure in January 1938, using it as a library and for art exhibitions, lectures, and musical programs. In that same year the Garden Club of Palm Beach held its annual flower show in the building, beginning the close association between the two groups and leading to the creation of the Four Arts Gardens.

The third cultural institution founded in this era, the Norton Gallery and School of Art, was a 1940 gift of Ralph Hubbard Norton, president of the Acme Steel Company of Chicago, and his wife Elizabeth Calhoun Norton. They gave the gallery building with an endowment to the community to serve as a permanent home for their extensive collection of paintings and sculptures, which included works by Copley, Gainsborough, Lely, Renoir, Reynolds, Utrillo, and Picasso, as well as paintings by the major American artists of the late nineteenth and early twentieth centuries. One of the most notable paintings in the collection, "Agony in the Garden," depicts a startling red-haired Christ, a self-portrait by Paul Gauguin.

Marion Sims Wyeth designed the new gallery placed in Pioneer Park on South Olive Avenue in West Palm Beach. It opened in February 1941 with over 100 paintings from the Norton Collection.

CHAPTER VI

Herb Roth's cartoons in the Delray Beach News *commented wryly on the changes brought about in a quiet resort area by the arrival of several thousand young servicemen during World War II. Courtesy, Delray Beach Historical Society*

The War and Postwar Years

*T*he Second World War brought far-reaching
changes to Palm Beach County. The establish-
ment of air bases at West Palm Beach and
Boca Raton resulted in large-scale construc-
tion, reviving that depressed industry. During
the course of the war the Army stationed tens
of thousands of troops at these and nearby bases,
including a small camp at the inlet and a camp
just across the Martin County line near Jupi-
ter. Without question, the troops created an
immediate economic impact on the area, but
the long-range effect of the military personnel
in Palm Beach County was even greater. Many
returned to the area after the war, seeking jobs
in the sunshine, and many more retired to
communities they first knew as soldiers.

The Army Air Corps established the two
county bases because small airports already
existed in both locations. The West Palm
Beach field resulted from the efforts of Grace
K. Morrison, secretary for the architectural
firm of Treanor and Fatio. Morrison had taken
flying lessons at the small private Belvedere
airport in West Palm Beach. After her first
solo flight in 1932 she became convinced that
the Palm Beaches needed a large public airport
with paved all-weather runways to allow regu-
larly scheduled passenger and airmail service.
To promote this cause she formed the Palm
Beach County Airport Association, which im-
mediately gained the active support of numer-
ous business and professional people in West
Palm Beach and many leaders of Palm Beach
society. As president of the association Morri-
son persuaded Maurice Fatio, John L. Volk,
Mrs. Frederick E. Guest, Mrs. Alfred G. Kay,
Mayor John Shepard, and Hugh Dillman to
serve on a committee to raise funds for the air-
port.

In January 1933 the association purchased
440 acres south of the old airport between Bel-
vedere Road and Southern Boulevard and se-
cured an overall design for the field. Morrison
then went to Washington where she gained a
$30,000 grant from the Civil Works Adminis-
tration, which supplied the labor to clear, drain,
and grade the four 3,000-foot runways. An ap-
plication to the Works Progress Administration
(WPA) secured an allotment of $108,071 in
July 1935. This amount, supplemented by

Standing in the center in her flying gear is Grace K. Morrison, the guiding force in the funding and design of the county's first public airport. She died in an automobile accident, just as the facilities were coming to completion in 1936. Courtesy, HSPBC

$19,595 in material and equipment from Palm Beach County, went for shell-and-oil paving of the runways and a 1,500-foot taxi strip. The association also built a small wooden administration building that contained offices, a waiting room, and the weather bureau's teletype service.

In September 1936, just three months before the airport opened, Morrison died in an automobile accident. The local newspapers and the members of the airport association spearheaded a campaign to name the airport in her honor.

The county commission approved and on December 19, when Eastern Air Lines inaugurated regular service, the new airport was dedicated as Morrison Field.

The Boca Raton airport came about through the efforts of A.B. McMullen, a pioneer Florida flier. Recognizing the importance of the air industry for state development and tourism, the 1933 Florida legislature created an Aviation Division within the State Road Department and named McMullen as its director. In a ten-year plan for development, he targeted Boca Raton as an area especially in need of an airport because the terrain afforded no natural areas for emergency landings, which were fairly common for the planes of that era. At the same time several members of the Boca Raton Club who owned airplanes asked the club management to provide a convenient landing field.

McMullen saw the possibilities of combining

Morrison Field was developed with local initiative and WPA funds. Eastern Airlines flew the facility's first commercial flight in December 1936. Courtesy, HSPBC

airport building with the national government's emergency relief activities, so he encouraged the club to ask the town to build an airport. What Clarence Geist wanted for his club he usually got; after all, the people of Boca Raton were largely dependent on him for their living. Gordon B. Anderson, general manager of the club, organized and planned the airport project, choosing a location northwest of the town on property with delinquent taxes. Boca Raton officials began condemnation proceedings while McMullen wrote the request for federal relief funds. After the town agreed to contribute $11,869 for the project, the WPA granted $38,537.

The use of WPA funds for construction of the airport required careful planning, since WPA projects were to provide work for individuals on relief, and although few citizens of Boca Raton or the surrounding communities were wealthy in this period, few were on relief. Thus the shortage of workers required the town

administration to postpone other proposed WPA projects, such as playground and beach development. Clearing and grading began in late 1936 with the grass runways completed in time for the 1937 season.

Shortly after the start of World War II in Europe the United States began a massive defense build-up. In one of the earliest projects Morrison Field was converted from a civilian airport to a military base. Construction began in November 1940, and the airport officially became a military post on February 28 when Lieutenant Colonel John Monahan arrived from Langley Field in Virginia to take command of the West Palm Beach facility. Sched-

As wife of the Commander in Chief, Eleanor Roosevelt toured stateside bases throughout the war. In Palm Beach County, she flew into Morrison Field and visited casualties being treated at The Breakers, which served as a hospital for the duration. Courtesy, HSPBC

uled airline flights and private planes continued to use the airport until a new auxiliary field six miles south at Lantana was completed. By the time the Japanese attacked Pearl Harbor, Morrison Field had been expanded to over 1,000 acres and was prepared, as "the most strategically situated" base in the southeastern United States, to protect the nation in case of a southern attack.

A month after Pearl Harbor, Morrison Field became part of the Air Transport Command with the mission of processing aircraft and air personnel for overseas duty. The height of wartime activity at the base came during an eight-month period prior to the Normandy invasion when 6,216 airplanes and 45,344 personnel passed through the field on the way to the European theater. Similar activity prior to the invasions of Italy and North Africa reflected the importance of Morrison Field on the European air route through the Caribbean, South America, and Africa. The West Palm Beach base also served as a way station for flights through South America to the Far East. One of its missions became the "Pipeline Project" of maintaining the 200 C-54 Skymasters used to transport critical war materiel over the famous Himalayan "Hump" in the China-Burma-India theater.

As victory in Europe neared, Morrison Field served as a center for the redeployment of tactical aircraft and military personnel to the Pacific theaters. In the last year of the war the base also became the home of the "Carasawl" route, the name deriving from Caribbean and South Atlantic Wing line. Transporting everything from vital military supplies to locomotives and chemicals used in hydroponic gardening projects, the Carasawl operations covered runs of 6,500 miles to South America, the Canal Zone, Ascension Island, Africa, Arabia, Italy, France, the Azores, and Bermuda.

On return flights the Carasawl line often carried wounded servicemen to American hospitals. One such hospital was on the oceanfront in Palm Beach. The luxurious Breakers Hotel joined the war effort as Ream Army Hospital and became noted for its occupational therapy division. In March 1944 Eleanor Roosevelt flew into Morrison Field on a visit to Ream Hospital, where she greeted patients and signed autographs. The newspapers reported that the first lady's stop was "a great morale booster."

Morrison Field also served as home for the 308th Reconnaissance Weather Group, which trained several weather squadrons for overseas duty. The group made history in 1946 when one of its B-29 crews became the first to fly

above a tropical hurricane. Invaluable weather data came from this flight, which proved that high altitude airplanes could track hurricanes and remove much of the uncertainty from predicting their paths and intensity.

When the United States entered World War II, the uses of radar as a military weapon were still in the development stage. Although a technical school had been established at Scott Field in Illinois, it became evident that a successful program required good flying weather throughout the year, proximity to the ocean (so shipping lanes could provide targets for practice runs), and relative security from the enemy. Boca Raton, with its small airport, seemed to fulfill these requirements, and it was close to Camp Murphy on the old Jupiter reservation, the site of the Signal Corps radar school. Army officials believed it advantageous that the Air Corps radar school be built nearby.

Starting with the Boca Raton airport, the Army acquired a total of 5,860 acres from more than 100 property owners. More than fifty families lived on the land, many of Japanese ancestry from the former Yamato colony. On the East Coast the government never confined the Japanese to camps. Many did lose their land to the air base, as did a black community of houses and shanties which, according to one source, "had been built over a period of fifteen years on land not possessed through legal channels."

Construction started in the spring of 1942, and with typical wartime speed the base opened for its first class in October, with 800 buildings completed by January of the next year. The project required over nine million dollars for construction of buildings and runways. At this time the Army Air Corps also took over the Boca Raton Club to house some of its thousands of trainees. The antiques, oriental rugs, and other elegant furnishings went into storage to be replaced by standard GI bunks and furniture.

Today one small runway remains as the Boca Raton Airport; the rest of the air base is covered by the campus of Florida Atlantic University. During World War II this was a major training facility for Army Air Corps radar operators. Courtesy, Boca Raton Historical Society

As the Army Air Corps' only radar training school during World War II the camp offered classes for electronics and radar officers, as well as courses for enlisted men covering all related specializations. Beginning with 1,340 men in 1942-1943, the school served almost 15,000 the next year and enrolled 16,281 troops by 1945. As the curriculum developed and flight training came to play a larger role, the base received more and more aircraft. The base had only ten dilapidated bombers in October 1942, but by the war's end 100 airplanes, half of them B-17s, were assigned to the field. The air base dwarfed the little town of Boca Raton, which was unable to supply enough civilian employees. When the number of civilians working at the facility rose to 1,500, they were drawn from communities as far away as Fort Lauderdale.

When the war ended, activities at Morrison Field and the Boca Raton base quickly diminished. On July 1, 1947, Morrison Field was placed on "de-militarized" status; operations of the Air Transport Command were transferred to a base in Mobile, Alabama. In that same year radar training activities moved to Keesler Field in Mississippi, hastened when 155-mile-

an-hour hurricane winds struck the base on September 17 and caused more than three million dollars in damage.

Palm Beach County had two additional military installations during the war years. The Army established a small base called Camp Higgins to guard the Palm Beach Inlet. The port itself was also taken over by the military. On the other side of the county in Belle Glade, the Army built a small work camp next to the Everglades Experiment Station in March 1945 for German prisoners of war. The Army brought the POWs to the area because the American draft had produced a shortage of agricultural workers.

A few weeks after the first prisoners arrived at the Belle Glade camp, they organized a strike to protest cuts in their cigarette ration. The strike occurred just as Allied troops were discovering the horrors of the German concentration camps. The unfavorable publicity given the strike by local newspapers contributed to a congressional investigation of Army handling (some said coddling) of the POWs.

Although the actual fighting in World War II never reached American shores, it reached to just offshore for Palm Beach County. Soon after the United States entered the war, the German navy began U-boat attacks in the

In the spring of 1942, German submarines torpedoed at least a dozen Allied ships in waters off the Florida coast. Several oil tankers were hit and burned within sight of county beaches. Courtesy, HSPBC

shipping lanes of the Florida Straits. The first sinking in Florida waters occurred off Cape Canaveral on February 19, 1942, when a German submarine torpedoed the tanker *Pan Massachusetts,* which was carrying 100,000 barrels of oil. Just two days later the tankers *Republic* and *Cities Service Empire* went down at Hobe Sound. The next day off Palm Beach the huge tanker *W.D. Anderson,* owned by the Atlantic Refining Company, exploded in a sheet of flames visible to residents from shore. Of the thirty-six-man crew, only one survived.

Many of the attacks came at night when the U-boats could see the ships silhouetted by the bright shore lights. While Miami Beach tourist interests fought blackout and dimout orders for months, Palm Beach observed its first complete blackout in early January 1942. Town officials reported "100 percent cooperation from every resident in Palm Beach." However, the sinkings continued.

May 4, 1942, began "the deadliest week off

The Duke and Duchess of Windsor first visited Palm Beach together when he was Governor General of the Bahamas during the Second World War. They frequently returned as guests of Robert Young, the New York Central Railroad president. The Duchess' uncle, S. Warfield Davies, had been president of Seaboard Air Line Railways in 1925 when it began service in the county. Courtesy, HSPBC

Palm Beach County," in the words of *Palm Beach Post* writer Bill McGoun, as the British tanker *Eclipse,* with a cargo of aviation fuel, received a direct hit about a mile offshore from Boynton Beach. Before the week ended, seven ships had been torpedoed, including the cargo carrier *DeIsle* and the tankers *Java Arrow, Lubrafol, Amazonas, Halsey,* and *Ohioan.* The loss of the tankers and their precious cargoes in addition to the terrible loss of life convinced officials to take further protective measures. The nation's first Civil Air Patrol squadron, based at the Lantana airport, began searching coastal waters for enemy submarines. A coast guard unit housed at the old polo fields at Gulf Stream inaugurated mounted night patrols of the beaches with guard dogs. A network of sixty spotter stations, placed in specially constructed towers or oceanfront buildings, kept a constant watch on the shipping lanes.

The Gulf Sea Frontier, charged with the defense of the Florida coast as well as the Bahamas and Cuba, had only three coastal cutters at Key West when the war began, along with several other inadequate ships and a few battered airplanes. As a result of the sinkings off Florida, concerned military officials made available more planes and vessels, which were organized into efficient "killer packs" that destroyed two U-boats during the summer of 1942. The increased vigilance of American defenders and German reassignment of their submarines to the North Atlantic ended the attacks off the Florida coast by the summer of 1943.

During the war years the civilian population of Palm Beach County supported the American cause with its money, time, and talents. In only two years after its founding in 1942, seventy-eight volunteers of the local Office of Civilian Defense donated 76,500 hours of work. The fourth war-loan fund drive raised $17,680,000 in the county. In 1944 the Community Chest and National War Fund drives were combined

During World War II thousands of service personnel found Palm Beach County a congenial duty station. Cartoon by Herb Roth. Courtesy, Delray Beach Historical Society

in the Palm Beaches; West Palm Beach contributed $36,445 and Palm Beach $51,647. On both sides of the lake volunteers staffed USO Service Centers, formed Motor Corps to deliver sewing, knitting, and surgical dressings for the Red Cross, and entertained off-duty troops in their homes and clubs. The Everglades Club held informal Monday night entertainments, democratically inviting officers and enlisted men on alternating weeks.

The top social names of Palm Beach organized Volunteers for Victory, with Mrs. Henry R. Rea as chairperson and Hugh Dillman as president, to coordinate all activities "for the comfort, entertainment, and morale of the American forces." The V for V opened offices in the Paramount Theatre and organized a 250-member knitting army, a recreational committee to furnish books, magazines, and games

to the clubrooms at Morrison Field, a Nurses Aid group to work as volunteers at local hospitals, and a transportation committee to drive area troops on sight-seeing expeditions and to the beaches. The V for V also opened and staffed a Soldiers' Bath House at the beach, where for only five cents the soldier received a towel and could check his valuables. The bathhouse also collected 100 swimsuits for loan to those who arrived without their own. More than 350 sol-

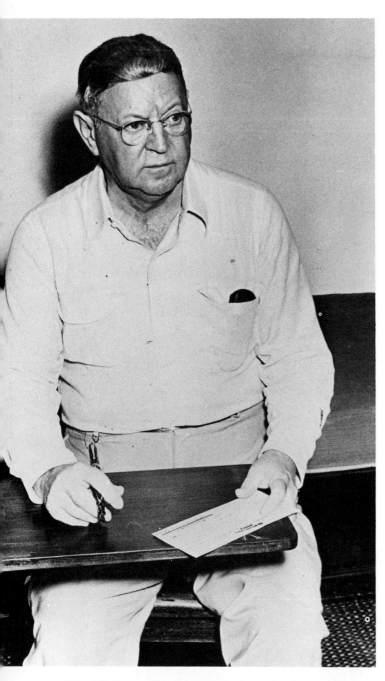

John H. Perry, Sr., bought the Palm Beach Post-Times in 1947 from the estate of Colonel E.R. Bradley for $1,050,000. He eventually acquired twenty-five newspapers in the state of Florida, receiving national attention because of the more than 6,000 weekly papers that depended on his Western Newspaper Union features syndication. Courtesy, Palm Beach Post-Times

diers made use of the bathhouse on typical summer Sundays before the war's end.

In the years immediately following the war, many changes occurred in the Palm Beaches. Perhaps one of the most far-reaching was the death of Edward R. Bradley on August 15, 1946. When ill health forced Bradley to close the Beach Club at the end of the 1945 season, it had been a Palm Beach institution for forty-eight years. Joseph P. Kennedy observed: "The zipperoo has gone out of the place." The simple white frame building was razed in the summer of 1947 after the furnishings were sold at auction. Bradley willed the casino grounds to Palm Beach for a public park.

Bradley had used his gambling profits to acquire various Palm Beach and West Palm Beach properties, including two newspapers. He came by these during the early years of the depression when D.H. Conkling, founder of the *Palm Beach Post* in 1908, and Sheriff Robert Baker, owner of the *Palm Beach Times* (started by Frank P. Fildes in 1922), decided to join forces. Since both newspapers had suffered several bad years, they jointly borrowed $100,000 from Bradley to continue publication. When the financial picture of the newspapers failed to improve, Bradley assumed ownership in 1934 and named C. Barry Shannon, his long-time business associate, as publisher. Shannon received the newspapers under Bradley's will, but only a few months after Bradley's death, Shannon also died. The newspapers found a new owner early in 1947 when long-time Palm Beach resident John Holliday Perry, Sr., purchased them for $1,050,000.

Perry owned a Florida newspaper chain of six dailies and fifteen weeklies that he started in 1922 with the *Jacksonville Journal*. Perry paid homage to his adopted state in 1925 when he asked Frank Parker Stockbridge to coauthor a book "to tell the true story of Florida." *Florida in the Making*, published the following year with an introduction by Governor John

The staff of the Palm Beach Daily News *posed in a gumbo limbo tree in 1910. The owner R.O. Davies stands at the bottom, and on the highest perch is Miss Ruby Edna Pierce, age 22. "Miss Ruby," seen in a more formal pose above, was recruited from her Sunday school class by Davies. After a year as cashier and another year as business manager of the little paper, she became the editor from 1910 until 1954. During her forty-four years, "The Shiny Sheet" was the voice of respectable society news in the resort life of the community. Courtesy, HSPBC*

W. Martin, became a national best seller.

In 1948 Perry also purchased the *Palm Beach Daily News* and the society magazine *Palm Beach Life* from Oscar G. Davies. Davies' father, Richard Overend Davies, had founded the magazine and bought the old *Lake Worth News* from Bobo Dean in 1905 with the silent backing of Henry Flagler. In 1907 the senior Davies hired Ruby Edna Pierce, who by 1910 had become editor and general manager of the *Palm Beach Daily News* and *Palm Beach Life* and continued to hold these posts until her retirement in 1954—certainly one of the longest

careers in Florida journalism.

After Perry's death in 1952, his son John Perry, Jr., continued to manage the Florida newspaper chain but eventually became more interested in building marine-research submarines. In June 1969 Cox Enterprises purchased all of his Palm Beach and West Palm Beach interests for an estimated twenty million dollars. James M. Cox, a former Ohio governor and Democratic presidential candidate in 1920, first entered the Florida newspaper scene in the early 1920s with the *Miami News.* The national newspaper chain he built is today a vast media empire that includes twenty daily newspapers as well as radio and television stations.

Bradley also owned the Embassy Club and the Spanish Provincial apartments on Royal Palm Way. Bryon D. Miller, who served as a vice president of the Society of the Four Arts, purchased both buildings in 1947 and then sold the club to the society for only $137,500. He included in the sale a sizable portion of valuable lakefront property. The Embassy, designed by Addison Mizner, had been used as a private nightclub. John L. Volk, who became architect for the conversion of the club into an art museum, enclosed the large patio and its outdoor dance floor to create a 1,000-seat auditorium and remodeled the other major rooms into gallery space. The addition of the Embassy allowed the older society building to be used entirely as a library.

Another major change of this period came as a result of the further lengthening of the Palm Beach season, ushering in the "barefoot" era. Resorters who spent most of the year in town called for greater informality in their activities and less pretentious surroundings. Many of the old Spanish-style villas suffered insensitive remodelings, and some were even divided into several houses. Moreover, the heat of south Florida summers demanded air conditioning. Many owners of large oceanfront estates came to see their houses as anachronisms, too large to air condition, impossible to staff adequately, and out of step with resort life.

Some owners, like Mrs. Horace Dodge, attempted to save their houses through rezoning to allow use as a club or school. Town officials usually refused such requests. Within a decade some of the greatest Mizner and Wyeth showplaces of the early 1920s fell under the wrecker's ball. In just a few short years new housing

subdivisions and even low-rise condominiums began to replace the former great estates.

The era's most sensational event was the disappearance of senior circuit court judge Curtis E. Chillingworth and his wife Marjorie in June 1955. Chillingworth, son of the pioneer attorney, received appointment to the court in June 1923 at the age of twenty-seven. When he disappeared from his oceanfront house in Manalapan, he had served on the court for thirty-two years. Although authorities found blood on the beach stairs and footprints leading to the sea, no further trace of the judge or his wife was found.

The disappearance remained Palm Beach County's greatest mystery until the fall of 1960 when Floyd Holzapfel, a petty hoodlum, confessed to their murders. Holzapfel said he and Bobby Lincoln, a small-time black gambler and moonshiner, were paid $2,000 by former West Palm Beach municipal judge Joseph A. Peel, Jr., to kill the circuit judge. According to Holzapfel, Peel feared that Chillingworth planned to have him disbarred for running a bolita gambling racket. The two killers took a small boat to the Manalapan house, kidnapped the judge and his wife, and threw them into the sea, weighted with heavy chains.

Holzapfel claimed that after the drowning of the Chillingworths, Peel also attempted to arrange the murder of state attorney Phillip D. O'Connell. O'Connell, still state attorney in 1961, prosecuted Peel for the murder of Judge Chillingworth. A weeping Holzapfel told the court that "people who have done what Joe Lincoln and I have done should be stamped out like cockroaches, not allowed to live." The jury, finding Peel guilty, recommended a life sentence. After serving almost twenty years of his sentence, dying of cancer, he received parole. Holzapfel, on the other hand, pleaded guilty to the murder and cooperated in Peel's prosecution. He received the sentence of death in the electric chair.

Although Palm Beach County remained largely undeveloped throughout the 1950s (in 1960 it had less than a quarter-million people), already some citizens complained that it had lost the natural unspoiled quality of earlier years. One of these, the novelist Theodore Pratt, had moved to Lake Worth from New York City in 1934 because he believed a serious writer needed isolation and peace. He found delight in the subtropical nature and simplicity of the leisurely life in prewar south Florida.

When Lake Worth "began to grow" after the war, Pratt moved to the Old Floresta section of Boca Raton. Old Floresta, a subdivision planned by Mizner in the mid-1920s, was a heavily wooded area several miles west of the town. Only one narrow road connected the twenty-nine Mizner-designed bungalows with the rest of the town. Pratt spent the next twelve years in Old Floresta writing the books about Florida on which his reputation rests.

His best-known work, *The Barefoot Mailman,* tells the story of the pioneer mail carriers and is the first of a Florida trilogy that recounts Palm Beach County history from pioneer days through the land boom and bust of the 1920s. The trilogy also reflects Pratt's personal aversion for what he saw as the new Florida. *The Barefoot Mailman* is set in the era when Florida remained an Eden, unspoiled by civilization. In *The Flame Tree* the snake enters the garden in the form of Flagler and the Florida East Coast Railway, bringing hordes of people, and they bring decline. In the final volume, *The Big Bubble,* a fictionalized account of Addison Mizner and his Boca Raton development, the great land boom of the twenties destroys Eden.

In 1957, still seeking his paradise away from civilization, Pratt moved to western Delray Beach. He said that Boca Raton had "exploded with real estate developments." In an article written for the *Miami Herald* Pratt said he en-

Theodore Pratt was the foremost author to settle in and write about Palm Beach County. His trilogy—The Barefoot Mailman (1943), The Flame Tree (1950), and The Big Bubble (1951)—focused on the historical evolution of the county from 1870 to 1930. By the early 1950s, Pratt was quite out of sympathy with the pace of progress. Courtesy, HSPBC

visioned the entire state turning into one great metropolitan area. The article, entitled "I Am a Fugitive from Florida's Progress," concluded that this "Floridapolis" might well find Pratt "marching through Georgia" to escape.

Unlike Pratt, most Palm Beach County residents welcomed the new urbanization. As its leaders once more promoted greater growth and development, it could no longer remain the peaceful resort county of that earlier day.

CHAPTER VII

*During the Kennedy administration, Palm Beach regained
a bit of its glamor as a prestige international dateline.
The Kennedy clan's association with the island resort
went back to the days when JFK was a toddler. Here
the First Couple are seen at a charity fund-raising ball.
Courtesy, HSPBC*

The Metropolitan County

*T*o many Palm Beach County residents no
ent more clearly illustrated the area's mod-
n character and growing prominence than
hn F. Kennedy's election to the presidency in
60. President Kennedy's parents, as owners
a Mizner-designed villa on the oceanfront in
lm Beach since 1933, and the new president
d been a part of Palm Beach life for over
ree decades. His pre-inaugural visit and year-
Christmas vacations with his family brought
world spotlight to bear on the county, which
thin just a quarter of a century had more
an tripled its population. An influx of middle-
d upper-income retirees, seeking the good life,
ompted developers to build new subdivisions
d cities. At the same time small specialized
sinesses, many involved in electronics, joined
dustrial giants like Pratt-Whitney and IBM
establish Palm Beach County plants.
Over the years, beginning with the sixty-
ree-year-old Henry M. Flagler's decision to
tend his railroad to Palm Beach in 1893, a
ttern for area development had emerged in
e work of his successors—Kelsey, Singer,
:ist, and others. Like Flagler they were men

of mature years who had made or inherited
large fortunes. They came to Florida for relax-
ation or retirement and soon found themselves
actively involved in development. This pattern
continued in the postwar period when John D.
MacArthur and Arthur Vining Davis became
interested in Palm Beach County.

MacArthur's involvement in Florida real estate resulted from his foreclosing in 1955 on a
large loan made to a developer. In the same
year he purchased the original Kelsey property
of 2,600 acres for five-and-a-half million dollars.
MacArthur had made his immense fortune
(close to three billion dollars by one estimate)
in insurance. The fourth son of a poor self-
ordained clergyman, he was born on March 6,
1897, in Pittston, Pennsylvania. All four Mac-
Arthur sons were highly successful. Alfred became president and principal stockholder of the
Central Standard Life Insurance Company,
Telfer built a publishing empire, and Charles,
a reporter turned playwright, wrote *The Front
Page* and *On the Twentieth Century.*

Perhaps because he was the youngest in this
highly competitive family, John MacArthur

John D. MacArthur was an eccentric insurance tycoon who enjoyed doing business from the corner table of the coffee shop of his Colonnades Hotel on Singer Island, just as seen in this picture. Eventually he became the largest property owner in the county. Courtesy, Palm Beach Post-Times

felt driven to succeed. Starting during the worst of the depression with borrowed capital, he acquired several bargain-priced insurance companies including Bankers Life and Casualty Company. Realizing that few people could afford conventional insurance coverage, he hit upon the idea of selling his policies through newspaper advertisements for premiums of only one dollar per month. He said, "Anyone can afford that. It will buy you $108 of insurance— enough to bury you." Working at first from an office in his apartment and the trunk of his car, with his second wife Catherine as his only employee, by 1943 MacArthur had made his first million.

From this time on the money gushed into the coffers of Bankers Life, which MacArthur owned outright. The newspaper campaign and the one-dollar-a-month policies increased the premium income from $46,195 in 1942 to $801,983 the next year. By 1953 premium income exceeded $100 million and reached almost $200 million by 1966. In that year MacArthur and Catherine left their modest Lake Park house of almost ten years and moved to an equally modest penthouse suite in the Colonnades Beach Hotel on Singer Island, which MacArthur had purchased in 1955. From an office in his suite, though more often from a Formica-topped table in a corner of the ho-

tel coffee shop, he directed the operations of Bankers Life and as many as twelve other insurance companies, in addition to his other holdings which included "the largest bank in Illinois outside of Chicago," the Alamo car rental company, television and radio stations (which at one time included West Palm Beach's Channel 12), a company that imported Mac-Arthur Scotch, and the development of thousands of acres of Florida real estate, much of it in Palm Beach County. In 1976 *Newsweek* reported that his real estate firms owned 100,000 acres in the state, making him Florida's largest landowner.

Lake Park, North Palm Beach, and especially Palm Beach Gardens became his major development projects. In 1962 RCA opened a $4-million plant to make computers in Palm Beach Gardens. Certainly the expansion pleased MacArthur, who happened to be a large RCA stockholder. In 1964 he also persuaded the Professional Golfers Association to move to Palm Beach Gardens, promising to build them golf courses and a clubhouse. Although the PGA's relationship with MacArthur ended in

Across Lake Worth from the city of North Palm Beach is John D. MacArthur Beach State Park. Part of the land was purchased by the state and county in 1980, and the remainder was donated by the MacArthur Foundation. Courtesy, Palm Beach Post-Times

1973, it later returned to different facilities in town.

MacArthur's love of a bargain meant he often purchased run-down property in which only he saw potential. He bought Palm Beach's old Biltmore Hotel in 1970 for one-and-a-half million dollars. Built as the Hotel Alba during the boom in 1926, it had never been a success. By 1970 most experts claimed it was ready for the wreckers. In 1977 MacArthur sold it to the developer Stanley Harte for $5,340,000. Harte in turn converted the old hotel into the luxurious Biltmore condominium, where one apartment can cost more than MacArthur paid for the entire building.

In 1976 *Newsweek* named MacArthur as the second wealthiest American (after shipping tycoon Daniel K. Ludwig). Nonetheless, he and

Catherine reportedly lived on less than $25,000 a year. Among the richest of the rich, he cultivated the image of the eccentric. He owned only two suits and usually wore a baggy sweater and no tie. He drank his own Scotch, for years rolled his own cigarettes, drove a beat-up car, and usually appeared unshaven. He collected left-over bread from the tables of the coffee shop to feed a flock of ducks on a nearby pond.

MacArthur claimed to be opposed to charity. According to William Hoffman in *The Stockholder,* MacArthur said, "Charity is for three types. Those who believe in God, those who want to be remembered when they're gone, and those who want to impress somebody. I'm an atheist, I hope people forget me, and if I want to impress anyone I'll paste the annual statement on the wall." Nonetheless, when he died on January 6, 1978, the world discovered he had placed most of his almost $3-billion fortune into the John D. and Catherine T. MacArthur Foundation, one of the nation's largest private charitable trusts. It has given millions to symphony orchestras, universities and colleges, and other conventional causes, but the MacArthur Foundation has become specifically associated with "genius grants" that allow individuals of exceptional talent the freedom to pursue research and writing free of normal responsibilities for a five-year period. Among those who have received the awards are Ada Louise Huxtable, formerly architectural critic of the *New York Times;* Ved Mehta, a *New Yorker* writer; William Kennedy, the Pulitzer Prize-winning novelist; and Robert Penn Warren.

Since its inception the foundation also has been generous to Palm Beach County. In 1980 it sold 206 acres on Singer Island just south of Lost Tree Village to the county for a little more than twenty-three million dollars and at the same time donated an eighty-two-acre tract, including a mile of oceanfront known as Air Force Beach. These 288 acres became the John D. MacArthur State Park, which preserves a large mangrove-surrounded lagoon that environmentalists consider one of the most important fish-supporting areas in Lake Worth.

In November 1985 the Foundation Land Company, the south Florida real estate arm of the foundation, agreed with regional water officials on a 16,570-acre private development that will preserve the 5,303 acres of the Loxahatchee Slough, the headwaters of the Loxahatchee River. The foundation's enormous wealth made possible the preservation of 47 percent of the land within the development. Considering that the Foundation Land Company owns as much as 25,000 additional acres in northern Palm Beach and southern Martin counties, environmentalists are optimistic about the prospects of responsible future development.

While John MacArthur purchased much of the north end of the county, Arthur Vining Davis claimed his territory at the south end. Davis became interested in Palm Beach County in 1956, when he paid J. Myer Schine twenty-two-and-a-half million dollars for the Boca Raton Hotel and Club and 1,500 acres of land in the town. In 1944 Schine, who owned several other hotels, including the Roney Plaza in Miami Beach, purchased the Boca Raton Hotel for two-and-a-half million dollars.

Davis was born the son of a Congregationalist clergyman on May 30, 1867, in Sharon, Massachusetts. After election to Phi Beta Kappa he graduated from Amherst College in 1888 and became one of the four original promoters of the fledgling Pittsburgh Reduction Company, which used the Charles Hall electrolysis process to produce aluminum. At age twenty-two Davis, "a cheeky little dynamo," talked Andrew Mellon into giving the small company a loan and buying some of its stock. By the time the Aluminum Corporation of America (Alcoa) was formed in 1907, the Mellons had bought a third of its shares. Davis

After a lifetime in the aluminum industry, having played a leading role in its vast expansion during World War II, Arthur Vining Davis dabbled in real estate, buying a home called Journey's End and an extra 100,000 acres or so in south Florida. In 1956 he bought the Boca Raton Hotel and Club with about 1,500 acres near the ocean. Courtesy, Boca Raton Historical Society

served on its board of directors and as its general manager. Davis eventually came to dominate the fast-growing company, and as its chairman he presided over the great expansion during World War II. At the end of the war Alcoa produced 90 percent of all virgin aluminum in the country.

Davis began spending winters in the Bahamas in the late 1930s. A pineapple-farming project on Eleuthera was followed by a similar

venture in south Dade County, and in 1949 Davis purchased Journey's End, a fifty-acre estate on Biscayne Bay, for his retirement. Unlike MacArthur, Davis willingly spent money to provide for his comfort. He paid thousands of dollars to remodel the house and $225,000 to reroute Old Cutler Road because the traffic noise kept him from sleeping.

In 1950 Davis cut most ties with Alcoa and moved to his Miami retirement house. Within a month he began purchasing great tracts of land and interests in a variety of concerns. His long-time secretary Evelyn Mitchell reminded Davis that he had planned to retire. Davis answered, "I can't retire. I've worked all my life. I wouldn't live six weeks if I quit."

By 1958 Davis owned 140,000 acres of land in Florida and the Bahamas. Like MacArthur he also held large investments in many companies. Unfortunately, by that year the postwar building boom had subsided and real estate values began to decline. According to Nixon Smiley, writing in the *Miami Herald*, Davis had spread himself too thin. Although *Fortune* had named him as one of the eight wealthiest Americans the year before, saying his fortune was between $400 million and $1 billion, in 1958 he needed money. He was ninety-one years old. Had he died in that year and his land been placed on the market, it could have meant disaster for Florida's economy.

To bring order to his holdings, Davis set up the Arvida Corporation, a public stock company that bears the first two letters of each of his

Top: *When Pratt-Whitney decided to come to Palm Beach County in 1956, the amount of "wilderness" available for jet-engine testing was one of the significant attractions. In twenty years the number of employees has grown from 1,000 to 7,600 in 1985. Courtesy, Pratt and Whitney Aircraft Group*

Bottom: *Arvida Corporation was formed in 1958 to coordinate the vast real estate interests of Arthur Vining Davis. Early development efforts of the company centered around the waterfront of Lake Boca Raton, where in the late 1960s the five condominiums and the twenty-story tower addition to the hotel went up. Courtesy, Palm Beach Post-Times*

names. He retained a 60 percent interest in the company and saw the public quickly bid the stock to twenty-four dollars a share. By the time of Davis' death on November 17, 1962, the new company had started to develop several Davis properties, including the Royal Palm Yacht and Country Club in Boca Raton.

Although reporters assumed *Fortune's* estimate of Davis' wealth was accurate, he refused to confirm it, asserting "It's none of your business." According to one story when he heard someone at a party call him the second richest man in America, he interjected, "That's not true, I'm fifth." After his death, court records showed he left a gross estate of $87,629,282. He gave away perhaps three or four million dollars in the last decade of his life to institutions like Miami's Baptist Hospital, Fairchild Garden, Amherst College, and the American School for Classical Studies in Athens, and he lost perhaps six million dollars when Castro took over his holdings on the Isle of Pines and perhaps a few million more from falling values of his Florida holdings. Nevertheless, his fortune had never come close to the *Fortune* estimate.

Since 1961 the chief executive officer of Arvida had been Brown L. Whatley, a "Southern gentleman" and president of the Jacksonville mortgage-banking firm Stockton, Whatley, Davin and Company. He continued as president after Davis' death, directing what one official called a "caretaker" operation. His very conservative management practices meant profits came from the sale of land, never from its development. In 1965 the Pennsylvania Railroad bought control of Arvida for six dollars per share, down considerably from its twenty-four-dollar high. Shortly afterward the Pennsylvania combined with the New York Central in the largest railroad merger in history, only to collapse in 1970 in the biggest bankruptcy in history.

Arvida was virtually untouched by the problems of the parent company, and its profits continued to rise every year. Whatley began a modest development program in Boca Raton that included four high-rise condominiums. Even though it lost money every year on the operation of the hotel, and its parent company remained bankrupt, Arvida officials committed millions of dollars to modernizing and refurbishing the old hotel building and constructing a new tower of modern guest rooms and a convention facility.

In 1971 Charles Cobb, a California developer, became Arvida's chief executive officer. He embarked on an aggressive development program in Palm Beach County that included the large Boca West complex, several other Boca Raton subdivisions, and a new oceanfront hotel called the Boca Beach Club. With the completion of the new hotel, Arvida replaced the old Cabana Club with a new condominium named the Addison, for Addison Mizner. In 1985 another new condominium called Mizner Court rose on the shores of Lake Boca Raton just north of the hotel. Since 1984 the Walt Disney organization has owned Arvida.

Palm Beach County also became the home of several large research and manufacturing companies that brought thousands of new jobs into the area. The first of the large companies was Pratt-Whitney, a division of United Aircraft, which decided in 1956 to build a multimillion dollar plant in a near-wilderness stretch of land northwest of West Palm Beach. The company chose the location for its aircraft engine development laboratory because it offered the isolation necessary to test very noisy jet engines, and because the mild winter climate attracted the scientists, engineers, and technicians needed by the industry. To secure a desirable site on the planned Bee-Line Highway, which county officials rushed to completion once Pratt-Whitney began construction, the company traded 9,000 acres to the south for 7,000 acres of the J.W. Corbett Wild Life Management area. Since the trade required legislative

Arriving in 1966 IBM bought 550 acres in Boca Raton, where its constantly expanding facilities today employ nearly 10,000. These Marcel Breuer-designed buildings were the home of IBM's personal computer efforts in the early 1980s. Courtesy, Palm Beach Post-Times

approval, Governor Leroy Collins included the project in his call for a special legislative session. The legislature approved, and the governor signed the act to transfer the property in September 1956.

When the $45-million facility officially opened in May 1958, the main plant covered 650,000 square feet and included experimental shops, offices, and a cafeteria. The engine testing area was built four miles to the west. The plant employed around 1,000 people at the time it opened, but by the end of 1958 that number had already doubled, and it continued to rise to a total of 7,600 in 1985.

By 1960 American Chlorophyll of Lake Worth was producing 8,000 pounds of the "amazing green element" a month, or 95 percent of all chlorophyll used in the United States. At the same time the sugar cane grown in the western section of the county was fast making Florida the nation's largest sugar producer. And while agriculture prospered, it was becoming clear that more and more of Palm Beach County's future lay with the new high-technology industries that built local plants.

Minneapolis-Honeywell opened a Semiconductor Research and Development Center in Riviera Beach to produce transistors. The plant was purchased in 1965 by Solitron Devices,

which has expanded it over the years. Both Siemens Communication Systems and Mitel opened Boca Raton plants, Motorola built in Boynton Beach, and RCA established a computer facility in Palm Beach Gardens.

In 1966 International Business Machines purchased 550 acres in Boca Raton from the Arvida Corporation. Although at first the company claimed the purchase was for "possible future expansion," when Thomas J. Watson, Jr., chairman of IBM, came to Boca Raton in March 1967 to host a breakfast for seventy-five area business leaders at the Boca Raton Hotel, he announced immediate construction of a 300,000-square-foot plant to manufacture the 360 Model 20 computer. He said that IBM chose Boca Raton over a California location because of climate, orange juice, the university, and the airport. Claude R. Kirk, Jr., the first Republican governor of Florida since Reconstruction, attended the breakfast as an adopted Palm Beach County citizen. Kirk had leased Duck's Nest, one of Palm Beach's oldest houses, as his private residence after his election in 1966. With a glass of Florida orange juice, Governor Kirk toasted then-California Governor Ronald Reagan's loss of the plant to the Sunshine State.

Even before the completion of its monumental Marcel Breuer-designed plant, IBM began manufacturing in leased quarters. From this start IBM became a giant presence in south Florida, employing 9,500 people in Palm Beach County alone. In August 1980 IBM decided to develop a micro-processor for home and business use. Where typically IBM took four to six years to launch a new product, a team of twelve people headed by electrical engineer Philip Estridge introduced the new IBM personal computer, or PC, in just eighteen months.

Estridge, who joined the company in 1959 after his graduation from the University of Florida, saw the PC go from a company sideline product to the centerpiece of IBM's automated office strategy. His innovative approach to marketing, the automated factory he developed in Boca Raton, and the clever ad campaign featuring a Charlie Chaplin-like character in a spotless white office, all contributed to the PC's skyrocketing sales. Estridge quickly rose from director of the development unit to president of the newly formed Entry Systems Division. In 1984 when sales of the PC totaled more than four-and-a-half billion dollars, he also became IBM vice president of worldwide manufacturing. Estridge had only recently been transferred to corporate headquarters in Armouk, New York, when he and his wife Mary Ann died in a Delta Airlines crash at Dallas on August 2, 1985. The same crash also took the lives of several other area residents, including Jane Thompson, assistant Palm Beach County administrator.

Industrial development and the growing population helped to bring change in racial relations in Palm Beach County. In 1954 the United States Supreme Court declared in *Brown v. Board of Education* that segregation of schools based solely on race deprived black children of equal educational opportunities. A year later the court told local school boards to admit children "on a racially non-discriminatory basis with all deliberate speed." According to *Like a Mighty Banyan, Contributions of Black People to the History of Palm Beach County,* this ruling had no effect on the local school system. In fact, two new high schools and Roosevelt Junior College were founded for all-black enrollment after the ruling.

Local black leaders recognized that the

During a distinguished career teaching at Roosevelt Junior College and Palm Beach Junior College, Dan Hendrix was elected in 1970 to the county school board. To date, he is the only black leader elected to a county-wide office. Courtesy, Palm Beach Post-Times

On March 31, 1978, friends and supporters congratulated Eva Mack (left) and Ruby Bullock on their election to the West Palm Beach city commission. Mrs. Mack was reelected in 1982 and became the first black to serve as mayor of West Palm Beach. Courtesy, Palm Beach Post-Times

school board planned to ignore the Brown decision and filed suit in 1956. The case *Holland and Holland v. Board of Public Instruction* dragged through the court system until 1966 when the school board was ordered to implement both faculty and student desegregation.

Although a few black students had attended white schools as early as 1961 under a "Freedom of Choice" option, only the specific court order brought plans to truly integrate the system. Nevertheless these plans proved a mixed blessing. According to *Like a Mighty Banyan,* "'integration' usually meant the phasing out of black schools and loss of the tradition and history associated with them and the demotion of black personnel."

Roosevelt Junior College opened its doors to county black students in 1958. At first students attended classes in the late afternoon and evening in the Roosevelt High School building, though later the junior college received its own building on 15th Street in West Palm Beach. Britton G. Sayles, principal of the high school, became the first and only president of the junior college. During the school's short existence, its enrollment reached 300, and over 100 students received associate in arts degrees. In 1964 the school became a branch of Palm Beach Junior College, but the next year the school board closed it entirely. Of the eighteen black faculty members of Roosevelt, only six received transfers to Palm Beach Junior College. One of these, Daniel Hendrix, became the first black member of the school board in 1970 and the first black to be elected to a county office.

Beginning in the 1960s, more and more blacks served in public offices and gained election to public positions. Riviera Beach, where the first black residents arrived in the pioneer period, elected a black attorney to its city council in 1962, and Bobbie Brooks became that city's first black mayor in 1975. Between 1971 and 1979 blacks held a majority of seats on the city council. Blacks have also won election to city councils in Belle Glade, South Bay, Delray Beach, Boynton Beach, and West Palm Beach. In the latter city Eva Mack was first elected to the city commission in 1978, and after winning reelection in 1982 she was chosen

by her fellow commissioners to serve as mayor.

On September 14, 1964, when local schools still remained largely segregated, a new state university in Boca Raton opened its doors to all upper-division students. Legislation in 1955 allowed the state university system to plan a new institution, which was to be placed in either Broward or Palm Beach County. The final choice of the site was made only after much persuasion. From the first a small group of civic leaders believed the air base in Boca Raton presented a logical site. State representative Ralph Blank of West Palm Beach proposed that Thomas F. Fleming, Jr., president of the First Bank and Trust Company of Boca Raton (now NCNB), organize a movement to lobby for the air base location.

Fleming devoted the next decade of his life to the cause of higher education in Florida. Although he was born in Georgia in 1916, Fleming's family had moved to Fort Lauderdale in 1924. He came to Boca Raton in 1941 after his marriage to Myrtle Butts to help manage the 4,000-acre Butts family farms, the largest vegetable growers in the area. He actively participated in the life of his adopted community from the first. To bring the new university to Boca Raton, Fleming discovered he had to persuade the city council to provide funds for maps, surveys, soil samples, and brochures; convince the state government that Boca Raton was the right location for the university; and win the federal government's agreement to donate the old air base site.

The projected million-dollar-per-week payroll and talk of the cultural advantages of an institution of higher learning gained a $500 appropriation from the city of Boca Raton, which local residents matched. The governing board of the state university system also approved the air base site when proponents pointed out that the central location on the Gold Coast placed 30,000 potential students within an hour's drive. Moreover, the size of the base and its

Thomas J. Fleming, Jr. (second from right), was the man most responsible for Florida Atlantic University being located in Boca Raton. To his right Governor Farris Bryant and the new university president Kenneth Williams join in the groundbreaking in 1962. Courtesy, Boca Raton Historical Society

The town hall in Palm Beach provides an appropriate backdrop for Memorial Fountain, designed by Addison Mizner, who established Mediterranean Revival as the fashionable style in the winter resort during the 1920s. Photos by Claudine Laabs

A wealth of architectural detail awaits the casual stroller in the Palm Beaches. The town hall was designed by the prolific firm of Harvey and Clarke, whose credits include virtually all the major buildings of pre-1980s West Palm Beach, except the Harvey Building.

Facing page: *The hexagonal lath house of the Royal Poinciana, the only portion of the hotel to survive demolition in 1935, and two views of the William J. McAneeny residence, designed by Maurice Fatio, recall the hotel and* palacio *eras. The lath house has been restored and lives on as an office and shopping complex. Photos by Claudine Laabs*

Facing page: *The original steeple of Bethesda-by-the-Sea and Jupiter Lighthouse date back to Palm Beach County's pioneer era, when the shores of Lake Worth were crowded only with jungle vegetation.*

This page, clockwise from top left: *The Palm Beaches of the 1980s bristle with major shopping malls, Phillips Point high-rises, and recreational boat traffic through the Palm Beach Inlet, at the West Palm Beach marina, and along the oceanfront. Photos by Claudine Laabs*

The hours of dawn and dusk blend tropical and urban colors around Lake Worth. Photos by Claudine Laabs

Facing page, top: *The Boca Raton Hotel and Club, born of the 1920s Florida land boom, entered a new phase of its history with construction of a twenty-story addition by the Arvida Corporation. Photo by Fred L. Eckel*

Facing page, bottom: *In the wake of this and other Arvida projects, Boca Raton has experienced a surge of development and population growth reminiscent of the town's first years. Photo by Harvey Olsen*

Left: *Conceived by Addison Mizner as a grand-scale luxury resort, the Boca Raton Hotel and Club ran into financial trouble when the land boom ended. It was purchased by Clarence Geist, who expanded the facility even beyond the original plans during the hard years of the depression. Photo by D.L. Kilcollins. Courtesy, Southern Stock Photos*

Below: *Polo is among the traditions continuing from Boca's origins as a resort for the social elite. Photo by Linda C. Olsen*

Facing page: *The oceanfront condominium has become a modern symbol for the good life in south Florida. Photo by Harvey Olsen*

This page: *Morikami Village is a legacy from one of the colonists of the Japanese agricultural settlement of Yamato. Photos by Linda C. Olsen*

Above and facing page, top: *The Loxahatchee Wildlife Reserve is an area for fishing, bird watching, and simple enjoyment of Florida wilderness. Photos by Harvey Olsen*

Facing page, bottom: *The wetlands offer unique vistas. Photo by Warren H. Flagler. Courtesy, Southern Stock Photos*

Pages 142-144: *Its scenic splendor remains a chief attraction of Palm Beach County for residents and visitors alike. Photos by Harvey Olsen*

President Lyndon B. Johnson received the first honorary degree given by Florida Atlantic University. In October 1964 he spoke at the dedication of the university, which was the first campus of the state university system in southeast Florida. Courtesy, Florida Atlantic University

promise for future expansion of the university impressed the board.

The action of the board, however, was only a recommendation to the state cabinet; before the cabinet could act the state needed clear title to the base with no restrictions on its use. Fleming enlisted the aid of George Smathers and Paul Rogers, who years before as students at the University of Florida had won election along with Fleming to Blue Key, the student leadership honorary. In 1960 Smathers was serving in the United States Senate and Rogers in the House of Representatives. Working through their offices, Fleming gained Civil Aeronautics Administration approval for a grant of 1,000 acres of land for the university free of all restrictions. A second grant of 203 acres called for the university system to run an airstrip for civilian aviation.

In the 1960 session of the state legislature an appropriation for planning money was blocked by members from north Florida, who called for a Pensacola site for the new university. Nonetheless, a cabinet grant of $260,000 funded a planning committee after the university system pointed out that by 1965 over 55,000 potential students would live on the southeast coast compared to less than 5,000 in the Pensacola area. The report of the committee called for an upper-division university of juniors, seniors, and graduate students with programs to dovetail with those of the junior colleges. It also called for extensive use of modern media equipment. The faculty, through the utilization of television and other aids, gained time for greater individual contact with students and for research.

In May 1960, after the state cabinet accepted the Boca Raton site, Fleming again took the lead in organizing private support for the university. A state bond issue in 1962 to finance buildings for all the state universities provided $5,300,000 to begin construction of the campus. In seeking a name for the university the board rejected the likes of Palm State, Peninsula, Kennedy of Florida, and A-Okay, finally settling on Florida Atlantic. Kenneth R. Williams, a Florida native and founding president of Miami-Dade Junior College, was appointed the first president of the new institution.

Through his involvement in fund-raising for Florida Atlantic, Fleming saw how inadequately the state supported higher education. Believing Florida needed a first-rate university system to attract clean, high-tech industry, he spearheaded a campaign for a $75-million bond issue to expand and improve higher education that won statewide approval in 1963.

As the buildings for the new university neared completion and the faculty and staff moved into their new offices and laboratories, it became increasingly evident that the state had failed to provide adequate funding to implement the innovative approaches to teaching outlined in the planning report. Moreover, hurricane Cleo struck the southeast Florida coast, postponing the university's opening a week to September 14, 1964. To add to the worries, enrollment was also much lower than projected.

The many problems plaguing the new university were forgotten when President Lyndon B. Johnson, in the midst of his reelection campaign, visited Boca Raton for the dedication ceremony. Fleming, who served as the president's Florida chairman, assured his presence to accept the university's first honorary degree. In his speech the president called for a "new revolution in education" that opened the doors of colleges and universities for all who could qualify. In his concluding remarks the president averred that he knew of "no limit to what a fully educated American public can do to enrich life in the next fifty years."

From fewer than 1,000 students in the first year, Florida Atlantic University has grown to over 10,000 students, who attend classes at the Boca Raton campus and in Fort Lauderdale, West Palm Beach, Belle Glade, and Fort Pierce. Florida Atlantic University, along with Marymount College, which opened in 1963 and became the College of Boca Raton in 1971, and Palm Beach Atlantic College, which opened in West Palm Beach in 1968, have all been instrumental in drawing new industry to the county.

If Charles Pierce could view the lake country from the top of the Jupiter Lighthouse in the 1980s, he would find that the silent, nearly deserted land he surveyed in 1872 has disappeared. The lake remains, though smaller now as bulkheads push ever outward to contain new roads and buildings. The dense forest surrounding the lake is gone, though much of Palm Beach County's great beauty still resides in its lush subtropical landscape. On the lake's

A sequence of Stevan Dohanos paintings depicting the route of the Barefoot Mailman hearkens back to the Palm Beach County that Charles Pierce knew in the pioneer era. Courtesy, HSPBC

western shore new skyscrapers like North-bridge Centre, Phillips Point, and Barnett Centre compete with new high-rise condominiums to dominate the skyline. To the west, gigantic shopping malls at Boca Raton, Boynton Beach, and West Palm Beach fill fields that formerly produced bumper bean and tomato crops, and even further west new subdivisions cover the former scrub pine land. New factories and laboratories, the agriculture and tourist industries, and the colleges and universities brought phenomenal growth. Charles Pierce might still have recognized some areas of the lake country in 1960. Then less than a quarter-million peo-

ple lived in the 2,023 square miles of the county. By 1985 its population had risen to 713,253, with projections of over a million by the turn of the century. Like most Palm Beach County residents, Charles Pierce would lament what had been lost, and look with confidence to the future.

CHAPTER IX

Partners in Progress

Palm Beach County's partners in progress are the men and women who transformed a tropical wilderness into a metropolitan county within a century. One hundred years ago pioneers existed on subsistence farming, fishing, and hunting along the Loxahatchee River and around Lake Worth.

The most significant event in the early progress of the county was the arrival of Henry Morrison Flagler's Florida East Coast Railway. The railroad brought skilled construction workers to the area to erect Flagler's resort hotels and oceanfront pier on the island of Palm Beach. The railroad also provided local farmers with their first reliable means for transporting produce to northern markets. Beginning with the incorporation of West Palm Beach, other communities emerged as railroad construction proceeded south.

Following World War I a speculative land boom invigorated business interests within the county. The older municipalities of West Palm Beach, Palm Beach, Delray, and Lake Worth were joined in the 1920s by Boynton Beach, Lantana, Pahokee, Riviera Beach, Kelsey City, Boca Raton, Jupiter, Greenacres City, Gulf Stream, and Belle Glade. During that same period the population of West Palm Beach tripled, and the county's largest city boasted highrise buildings, modern telephone service, a second railroad station, extensive boatyards, and a navigable seaport. In the 1930s the county's 50,000 residents gained a college, museums, and various cultural organizations.

During the 1950s Palm Beach County's population increased 100 percent as a wave of modern homesteaders necessitated the construction of mobile home parks, retirement subdivisions, resort facilities, public beaches, parks, and fishing piers, leading to the incorporation of fifteen new municipalities in the county within the decade.

In the years that followed, the arrival of communications, high-technology, light manufacturing, and defense-related industries attracted additional permanent residents. The rich Everglades agricultural area contributed produce, cattle, and sugar cane to the county's economic growth. Airports, expressways, and an expanded seaport provided the infrastructure for a modern metropolitan county.

The organizations whose stories are detailed on the following pages have chosen to support this important literary and civic project. They illustrate the variety of ways in which individuals and their businesses have contributed to the county's growth and development. The civic involvement of Palm Beach County's businesses, institutions of learning, and local government, in cooperation with its citizens, has made the area an excellent place to live and work.

The 1920s skyline of West Palm Beach took shape during the land boom; today it is being reshaped by the resurgence of business enterprise throughout Palm Beach County. Courtesy, HSPBC

HISTORICAL SOCIETY OF PALM BEACH COUNTY

The Historical Society of Palm Beach County was chartered in April 1937 in Palm Beach. Its honorary president, the Right Reverend Nathaniel Seymour Thomas of Bethesda-by-the-Sea Episcopal Church, donated his personal library of Palm Beach County and Florida history to the organization. Palm Beach Circuit Court Judge Curtis E. Chillingworth was elected the society's first president. Other early presidents included Palm Beach Mayor James M. Owens, Jr., Dr. Edmund L. Dow, Dr. George A. Waterman, John H. Morice, and Dr. Daniel J. McCarthy.

In 1940 the Florida Historical Society held its annual meeting at the Whitehall Hotel, where a temporary exhibit of Palm Beach County history and artifacts was displayed for the first time to a statewide audience. The following year the organization established an archive in the library of the Society of the Four Arts, designed by Treanor and Fatio and built in 1936 at Four Arts Plaza in Palm Beach.

Palm Beach Circuit Court Judge James R. Knott served as the so-

The vast resources from a 3,000-volume library of books and manuscripts to artifacts from south Florida Indian archaeology provide for hours of research by (left to right) Nan Dennison, director; Trudy Francis, volunteer; Grover C. Herring, president of the historical society from 1969 to 1972; and James A. Ponce, board of governors. Courtesy, The Image Group, Inc.

ciety's president from 1957 until 1969. In February 1960 the organization moved into Whitehall, the Henry Morrison Flagler Museum designed by architects Carrere and Hastings and built in 1901 in Palm Beach. Under Judge Knott's leadership the association assembled a large collection of artifacts and historical documents. Judge Knott's historical articles appeared in the "Brown Wrapper" of the Sunday *Palm Beach Post* beginning in January 1978.

Presidents of the Historical Society of Palm Beach County succeeding Judge Knott included Grover C. Herring, Arthur E. Barrow, James E. Watt, Edwin V. Pugh, Mary C. Linehan, Donald W. Curl, Linda M. Cothes, and Charles W. Potter. Maxine Banash, the association's first employed director who served from 1970 until 1984, was succeeded by Nan Dennison in October 1984.

The society's collections include a 3,000-volume library of books and manuscripts; the earliest periodical publications in Palm Beach County; area and regional maps, charts, and surveys; a vertical clipping file of local history items; and a photographic

Board members of the Historical Society of Palm Beach County are (top row, left to right): Julian Rowley, board of governors; the Honorable James R. Knott, president emeritus; the Honorable Charles W. Potter, president; professor Edwin V. Pugh, board of governors; Bertram M. Shapero, first vice-president; and the Honorable Harvey E. Oyer, board of governors. In the bottom row (left to right) are professor Donald W. Curl, secretary; Nan Dennison, director; Mary Linehan, second vice-president; Jean Matheson, board of governors; Lynn Butler, board of governors; and Alexandra Fatio Taylor, board of governors. Courtesy, The Image Group, Inc.

archive. The collection also contains original and microfilm copies of architectural tracings, drawings, and renderings by noted Palm Beach County architects. The organization's artifacts range from south Florida Indian archaeology finds to Addison Mizner furniture donated from Palm Beach estates.

The Historical Society of Palm Beach County publishes a newsletter, *The Sunlit Road*, six times per year. Once a month from November to April it sponsors a lecture program open to the general public on a historical topic of interest to Palm Beach County residents.

SUNPOINT SAVINGS BANK, FSB

Lake Worth Federal Savings and Loan Association received its charter in May 1937 from the Federal Home Loan Bank Board in Washington, D.C., as a locally managed and mutually owned thrift and home financing institution. Manager Roger E. "Mike" Branch, the only employee until January 1940, opened the association's first office in the Reanno Arcade building at Lake Avenue and Dixie Highway in Lake Worth. Robert S. Erskine was elected its first president by a board of directors that by 1939 included Erskine, L.T. McGee, E.G. Beane, Roy E. Garnett, and Roger E. Branch. These five men controlled the destiny of the Lake Worth Federal Savings and Loan Association for the next sixteen years.

In June 1939 the first government-secured Federal Housing Administration loan was financed. The million-dollar savings goal was reached in June 1944, but because home construction during World War II was nearly impossible, the institution invested in government bonds. In 1946 the association inaugurated the first government-insured Veterans Administration G.I. loans for Palm Beach County veterans.

By 1954 assets passed the $10-million mark. From this prosperity the association constructed its first building at Lake Avenue and Palmway, which opened in September 1956. An agency office was opened in Boynton Beach in September 1955, but initially only collections on mortgages and existing savings accounts were permitted under the charter. However, approval was finally secured from Washington to build the first branch, which opened in March 1959, on South Federal Highway in Boynton Beach.

Upon Robert S. Erskine's death in January 1957, vice-president Roger E. "Mike" Branch was elected the association's second president. In June 1958 approval was also secured to change the name from Lake Worth Federal Savings and Loan Association to First Federal Savings

Sunpoint Savings Bank Administrative Center, designed by architects Reynolds, Smith and Hills, opened in November 1977 on Tenth Avenue North in Lake Worth.

and Loan Association of Lake Worth, because the board planned to establish branches outside the town limits of Lake Worth. A second branch, on Lantana Road in Lantana, opened in December 1964. Three years later the association cooperated with the Historical Society of Palm Beach County to publish *Lure of the Sun: A Story of Palm Beach County.*

Branch retired in January 1970 and Ronald M. Finch, an employee since 1958 and vice-president since 1968, became the institution's third president. Under Finch's leadership nine additional branches were opened in the 1970s and five branches in the early 1980s. In November 1977 the association opened a four-story administrative center, designed by architects Reynolds, Smith and Hills of Jacksonville, on a nine-acre site on Tenth Avenue North, Lake Worth.

In February 1985 the association's name was changed to Sunpoint Savings Bank, FSB, to describe its new, expanded services and to more accurately reflect the south Florida geographic area it serves, with seventeen branches in Palm Beach, Broward, Martin, and St. Lucie counties.

FRAN MURPHY INTERIORS, INC.

Fran Murphy, a native of Virginia, moved to Tallahassee in 1950 and graduated from Florida State University with a degree in interior design. In 1963 she established her first design studio in the center of the fashionable Decorators' Row on Fortieth Street in Miami to service residential and commercial clients in Dade County. As her interior design business grew she was increasingly drawn to the luxury residences and commercial growth in Palm Beach County.

In 1974 Murphy moved her design operation from Miami to a 15,000-square-foot showroom at the corner of Clematis Street and Railroad Avenue in West Palm Beach. At that time Clematis Street was not considered an uptown location for a design firm; nevertheless, she envisioned the redevelopment possibilities for downtown West Palm Beach.

In September 1980 Murphy, as one of the owners, joined four investors and purchased the three-story Burdines department store on the northwest corner of Clematis Street and North Dixie Highway. The extensively remodeled 165,000-square-foot structure became the D&D Centre of the Palm Beaches. It opened in January 1981 as a decorators' and designers' center with elegant trade showrooms.

On the third floor of the center, Murphy created a 45,000-square-foot luxury showroom filled with outstanding collections of the finest contemporary furniture and accessory lines, displayed in an art gallery setting with dramatic lighting and silhouette elevations. The majority of the furniture displayed is from Italy, France, and the United States. In

The D&D Centre of the Palm Beaches is a decorators' and designers' center with elegant trade showrooms.

addition, the showroom features an outstanding collection of antique and modern sculpture and paintings. The facility also includes a carpeting department, a blueprint and photocopy department, a fabric and wallpaper library, and three private conference rooms for designer/client presenta-

---

Fran Murphy, president.

tions. The firm's staff, which includes a professional architect and ten interior designers, offers a full range of interior design services. The company also maintains a large warehouse inventory of furniture and decorator items for immediate delivery.

In August 1985 Murphy introduced her own line of electronic furniture for national distribution. The collection features electronically operated built-in component wall units

that are custom fitted for individual needs. These extravagant furnishings are finished in clear lacquer and contain ingeniously devised moving parts.

Murphy's three children all have worked in various aspects of the design industry: Michael Clark is an architect, Carol Murphy is an interior designer with the firm, and Tim Murphy worked in administration for Fran Murphy for five years.

Since 1977 Fran Murphy has maintained membership in the West Palm Beach Chamber of Commerce and is on the Economic Council of the Palm Beaches. She also serves on the management board of Flagler

A mother-of-pearl and penshell console on display at the D&D Centre.

National Bank and is a past president of the Downtown Association of West Palm Beach. Through Murphy's accomplishments in the design industry and her dedication to the redevelopment of downtown West Palm Beach, her D&D Centre of the Palm Beaches is acknowledged by her clients, her peers, and the international design press as one of the most successful trade showrooms in the country.

The unique D&D Centre of the Palm Beaches serves as a focus for the trade design district in the redevelopment of downtown West Palm Beach. It is the premier marketplace for designers, decorators, and architects in Palm Beach County. The facility also serves as headquarters for the Design Council of the Palm Beaches and the Palm Beach County Chapter of the American Institute of Architects.

The Fran Murphy Electronic Line. With just the push of a button, one can move an entire residence from clean, slick lacquer walls with curvilinear shapes into a high-tech audio video, entertainment world. A Fran Murphy creation, the walls are custom crafted for individual situations.

A faux marble pedestal with bust.

BANK OF PALM BEACH AND TRUST COMPANY

Constructed at the northwest corner of Cocoanut Row and Whitehall Way, on the grounds of the old botanical gardens of Henry M. Flagler's Royal Poinciana Hotel, the Bank of Palm Beach and Trust Company began operations on December 1, 1953. Lake Worth architect Edgar S. Wortman designed the colonial-style brick building with two drive-up windows. R.M. Newton of Bank Design, Inc., of New York, designed the air-conditioned interior with modern banking facilities: sixteen teller windows in the banking room, a directors' room, soundproof bookkeeping department, trust department, safe deposit department, and a security vault.

The bank, only the second to open in Palm Beach in a quarter-century, was formed by Palm Beach businessmen and residents to expand traditional banking services in a community that was then showing important signs of growth. Investment banker Thomas M. Cook was the founder and chairman of the board of directors of the new institution. The first president, Messmore Kendall, was succeeded by George E. Patterson from 1955 until 1960. John F. Nash served as president briefly during 1960, when the bank's working space was tripled by adding 12,000 square feet to the interior and two additional drive-up windows to meet increasing needs. York D. Hollingsworth, president from 1961 until 1969, offered full banking services as well as the new Golden Passbook and Checking accounts.

Hoke T. Maroon organized south Florida's first bank holding company, Commercial Bancorp, in 1965. Maroon purchased 95,000 shares, a majority of the stock, from chairman Cook and other directors of the bank

The Bank of Palm Beach and Trust Company's main office is located at 40 Cocoanut Row in Palm Beach.

in March 1966. The institution then became part of the holding company that soon after changed its name to Florida Commercial Banks, Inc. Although commanded by the holding company, which by 1971 owned controlling stock interest in six commercial banks in south Florida, the Bank of Palm Beach and Trust Company remains a separate corporate entity, operating with its own board of directors and a full complement of officers and employees.

James E. Morgan, Jr., joined the institution in 1957 and became its fifth president twelve years later. Following approval by the Florida legislature, six branches were established: Southdale (1978) in West Palm Beach, Oakbrook Square (1979) in Palm Beach Gardens, Century Corners (1981), South Dixie (1982) in West Palm Beach, Gardens Park Plaza (1985) in Palm Beach Gardens, and, most recently, Lakeshore Plaza, which opened in West Palm Beach in 1986.

RFD PATTEN, INC.

Beginning in 1939 Fred F. Patten pioneered the development of inflatable life rafts in the United States. At the outset of World War II the Navy's Bureau of Aeronautics adopted Patten's prototypes and commissioned him as an officer responsible for engineering and development of life-saving apparatuses.

Following the war and his release to inactive duty, he founded the Patten Company, Inc., in Worcester, Massachusetts, in 1947. The business manufactured inflatables for military aircraft. Through continued research and development the Patten Company became the major supplier of these products to the government.

In 1955 the Patten Company relocated to Lake Worth and erected a Quonset-type structure on Tenth Avenue North. The move from the northern climate was prompted by the possibility of static electricity which, in the presence of flammable materials, could cause a serious fire. The humid climate available in south Florida was more conducive to the enterprise.

During the 1960s Patten supplied life rafts to the Apollo and Skylab programs for the National Aeronau-

The Lake Worth site of the present manufacturing plant of RFD Patten, Inc.

tics and Space Administration. During the escalation of the Vietnam War, the firm produced thirty 20-man life rafts per day. From 1963 until 1973 it also manufactured Coast Guard-approved, life-saving equipment for passenger-carrying vessels.

In 1973 American Safety Equipment Corporation acquired Patten's

operations and moved to Miami the following year. Fred F. Patten, however, still held title to the Lake Worth site and its newly completed steel-frame manufacturing facility. In August 1974 Patten's sons, Robert and Stephen, along with former executives Joseph S. Sopczak and Frank J. Miller, reestablished the company at the Lake Worth site under the name Res-Q-Raft of Florida, Inc.

In 1978 a majority of the firm's stock was acquired by RFD Group, Ltd., of Godalming, Surrey, England, the leading firm for the research, development, and manufacture of inflatables in the United Kingdom. Fred F. Patten returned from retirement as chairman of the board and chief executive officer of the new entity, RFD Patten, Inc. In 1983 Stephen F. Patten became its president.

RFD Patten, Inc., hand-assembles rubber-coated nylon fabrics into inflatable one-, four-, seven-, twelve-, and twenty-man life rafts; life jackets; and bouyancy bags used in the installation of transoceanic telephone cables. The firm continues to be the leading supplier of inflatable life rafts for military aircraft in the United States.

RFD Patten, Inc., is under the direction of (left to right) Robert F. Patten, engineering; Fred F. Patten, director; and Stephen F. Patten, president.

FLAGLER NATIONAL BANK OF THE PALM BEACHES

Flagler National Bank of the Palm Beaches began operations in December 1974. At that time it was the first national bank to be chartered in West Palm Beach in thirty-eight years. Its first facility, located on South Flagler Drive, was a modest trailer with a lobby, vault, night depository, and three drive-in windows.

The institution was organized by local West Palm Beach business and professional leaders who included chairman of the board William C. Clark, president of Cornelius, Johnson and Clark; John E. Murphy, president of The Murphy Construction Company; attorney Phillip D. O'Connell, Sr., of O'Connell and Cooper; architect R. Carroll Peacock of Peacock and Lewis; and attorney A. Ward Wagner, Jr., of Cone, Wagner, Nugent, Johnson and McKeown. Thomas E. Rossin, attorney and veteran banker, was the first president of Flagler National Bank and Loren H. Hoeltke served as cashier. These seven gentlemen formed Flagler National's first board of directors, and by December 1975 total bank assets exceeded twelve million dollars.

Richard S. Johnson, chairman of Cornelius, Johnson and Clark, replaced Hoeltke as director in 1977 and, following Florida branch-

Flagler Center—headquarters for Flagler National Bank.

banking legislation, two branches were opened: Forest Hill Banking Center in West Palm Beach and Northlake Banking Center in Lake Park.

In June 1978 Flagler's downtown office moved from its trailer into Flagler Center. This six-story office facility was the first major commercial building to be constructed in

downtown West Palm Beach in over forty years.

Alex W. Dreyfoos, Jr., president of WPEC Channel 12, joined the board of directors in 1979. In July of the following year, the institution commissioned Robert Helsmoortel to design a sculpture of its logo, and the sculpture was installed at Flagler Center. By December total assets exceeded fifty-six million dollars.

The year 1980 also marked the beginning of the annual Holiday Boat Parade, an event sponsored and organized by the bank, in cooperation with the city of West Palm Beach, for the residents of Palm Beach County. This event draws thousands of spectators yearly to the shores of Lake Worth to view the many beautifully decorated yachts and the spectacular fireworks finale.

Growth continued as branches were established on Palm Beach Lakes Boulevard in West Palm Beach in 1980, on P.G.A. Boulevard in Palm Beach Gardens in 1981, in West Delray Beach in 1981, and in Lake Worth and Jupiter in 1982.

In 1983 the Flagler Bank Corporation was formed as the parent company of Flagler National Bank of the Palm Beaches. In 1984 the bank purchased the Boca Raton office of Colonial Trust Company, renaming it the Boca East Banking Center. By December total assets reached $201 million.

The year 1985 proved to be an exciting one with the opening of the new Operations Center in Riviera Beach, the County Complex Banking Center in downtown West Palm Beach, and the Boca North Banking Center in Boca Raton. Two new offices are planned for 1986 in downtown Delray Beach and on West Forest Hill Boulevard, which will bring Flagler National's total to thirteen banking centers serving Palm Beach County residents from Jupiter to Boca Raton.

Flagler Bank Corporation's board of directors are (left to right) R. Carroll Peacock; Alex W. Dreyfoos, Jr.; Phillip D. O'Connell, Sr.; William C. Clark, chairman; Richard S. Johnson, vice-chairman; A. Ward Wagner, Jr.; John E. Murphy; and Thomas E. Rossin, president and chief executive officer.

ST. MARY'S HOSPITAL

In the late 1930s a group of women in Palm Beach, led by Mrs. R. Stuyvesant Pierrepont, recognized the need for an extended care facility to treat the county's crippled and terminally ill. Alfred G. and Elizabeth D. Kay joined the group in selecting a site on Forty-fifth Street in West Palm Beach for what, in the planning stages, was named Convalescent House.

In January 1938 the founders met at St. Ann's Catholic Church and requested Father R.T. Bryant's assistance in contracting the Franciscan Sisters of Allegany, New York, who were then operating St. Francis Hospital in Miami Beach. A group directed by Mother Mary Damian Fitzpatrick came to West Palm Beach and agreed to open what would be known as St. Mary's Hospital.

St. Mary's, a nonprofit, Catholic, fifty-bed nursing home, was completed and opened in 1939. Edward R. Bradley, owner of the famous gambling casino in Palm Beach, donated funds to build a convent and chapel for the Franciscan Sisters to the north side of the main building.

St. Mary's had been open for less than a year when it became apparent that patients required a level of care not provided in a nursing home environment. In 1939 the facility became an acute care hospital.

West Palm Beach physician Wellington George, M.D., St. Mary's first chief of staff, organized a medical staff from members of the Palm Beach County Medical Society. In the early 1940s the addition of the four-story west wing and the creation of the medical staff were the real beginnings of St. Mary's as a comprehensive health care facility.

In 1947 Mother Fitzpatrick's assistant, Sister Josephine Marie Waters, O.S.F. (Order of St. Francis), was appointed the hospital's second administrator, serving until 1974. Con-

St. Mary's Hospital, designed by Henry K. Harding, opened in 1939.

struction of the south wing, housing obstetrics, pediatrics, and a 31-bed patient floor, was completed in 1947. Good Samaritan Hospital transferred ownership of Pine Ridge Hospital, which served West Palm Beach's black community, to St. Mary's in 1947. Pine Ridge Hospital was reorganized in 1956 to what is presently the north wing of the Franciscan Pavilion.

From 1947 until 1959, when vaccines were developed to prevent polio,

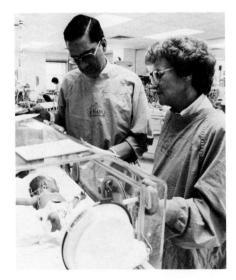

St. Mary's was one of three regional polio centers in Florida. From 1953 to 1962 the nursing school graduated 121 nurses. Following Sister Waters' retirement, Sister Gladys Sharkey served as interim administrator.

In November 1975 Thomas F. Hennessey was appointed the first lay chief executive officer of a Franciscan Sisters of Allegany hospital. The Sister Josephine Waters Pavilion was dedicated the following year, and the neonatal intensive care unit was initiated in 1978. In November 1983 John E. Fidler became the second lay chief executive officer at St. Mary's. In 1985 St. Mary's Hospital, a 382-bed facility, was providing a full range of medical and surgical services to all segments of the community.

Pastoral care associate Sister Joan Carberry, O.S.F., and chief of neonatology Luis Arango, M.D., observe an infant in the hospital's modern neonatal intensive care unit.

FIRST NATIONAL BANK IN PALM BEACH

First National Bank in Palm Beach opened December 1, 1927, on South County Road in Palm Beach in a Mediterranean-style building designed by the noted New York City and Palm Beach architectural firm of Treanor and Fatio. Veteran bank president Francis A. Shaughnessy financed the institution's first decade (1927-1937) through construction loans for Palm Beach's finest mansions. A most unique service, a climate-controlled warehouse, was provided for wealthy clientele to safeguard antiques, furs, paintings, and wine during the nonsocial season in this fashionable winter resort.

During its second decade president Wiley R. Reynolds, Sr., welcomed bank customers through electric-eye doors to an institution that offered an impressive list of personal banking services. A post office, telegraph office, and telephone directories of European capitals and principal U.S. cities were added conveniences. A travel bureau furnished a cosmopolitan clientele with international travel tickets, travelers' checks, and letters of credit.

Looking south at the First National Bank. By 1941 the bank occupied most of the buildings shown.

Introduced in June 1939, the technologically advanced Audichron machine was electrically programmed to answer eight incoming telephone calls with a recorded voice announcing the correct time, temperature, and advertising the most modern banking services. By January 1941 the Audichron was answering an average of 2,500 calls per day.

At the beginning of World War II First National was cited by *For-*

tune magazine for its progressive management. An Associated Press teletype machine kept customers apprised of the latest war developments and boosted sales to over eighty-one million dollars in government war bonds. Innovations during the bank's second decade also included check-sorting machines, electric typewriters, and an auto-teller window.

Wiley R. Reynolds, Jr., First National's president from 1947 until 1965, introduced air conditioning, automatic deposit of dividends by mail, stenographic services for vacationing businessmen, and a five-day work week. By the mid-1960s over

First National Bank in Palm Beach sold over eighty-one million dollars in government war bonds during World War II.

The bank's travel bureau provided many services for its international clientele.

half of the institution's employees, including eight officers, were women. An outdoor electric sign was installed to show the correct time and temperature to passing motorists.

Computer banking was introduced by William K. deVeer, president from 1965 to 1978. In 1973 a foreign currency department was instituted, and in February 1977, following approval by the Florida legislature, the South Ocean Office was opened in Palm Beach.

Beginning in 1978 the bank's fifth president, Thomas M. Keresey, led an expansion program with six new branches. The branches at Sunrise Avenue in Palm Beach (1979), Jupiter/Tequesta (1981), Boynton Beach (1981), and at the Royal Palm Plaza in Boca Raton (1984) established First National as a diversified countywide financial institution. In 1985 the bank opened a full-service office in Coral Gables in Dade County to provide international banking services. Palm Beach Capital Management, Inc., was established in August 1984 in Palm Beach to serve as an investment advisor for corporations, endowments, foundations, and institutions throughout Florida.

In 1980 First National Bank of Palm Beach, Inc., was incorporated and the following year became a registered bank holding company.

First National Bank in Palm Beach continues a tradition of providing modern, full-service personal, commercial, and trust banking services to the residents of Palm Beach County.

Actress Mary Pickford listens to the recorded time and temperature on the Audichron machine in 1948. Marketing director Robert E. Conn programmed the machine to advertise modern banking services.

161

DEXTER TOOL COMPANY

Three mechanical engineers, Pierre Deziel, Louis Deziel, and Paul Auger, founded Dexter Tool Company in September 1965 on South Street in West Palm Beach as a machine shop in support of Pratt & Whitney's Government Products Division's experimental requirements. The firm specialized in conventional machining of small to medium-size jet engine parts, accounting for $230,000 in sales in its first year of service.

The business was reformed in 1968, when Jack Biederwolf became an owner and president of Dexter Tool Company. It began to fulfill Pratt & Whitney's demand for larger and more complex parts including, but not limited to, seals, hubs, semi-finished disks, short shafts, turbine cases, and compressor cases.

In 1970 Dexter Tool Company moved to its present location on West Fifty-third Street in West Palm Beach. Between 1965 and 1978 the firm was a sophisticated aerospace engineering and manufacturing facility for prototype jet and rocket engine parts, with sales totaling two million dollars by 1978.

In 1978 John F. Over joined Dexter Tool Company and became its president the following year. Under his management the firm made a commitment to Pratt & Whitney's production as well as its prototype requirements, one of the few companies in the aerospace industry performing both functions. A separate building was erected to house the latest in CNC turning and milling centers, computers for programming, and electronic inspection equipment. The operations also include numerically controlled grinding equipment and automated welding equipment.

Dexter Tool Company manufactures approximately 650 parts including the major rotating and nonrotating parts of a gas turbine engine. By 1985 the firm had grown to 115 employees, producing more

John F. Over, president of Dexter Tool Company since 1979.

than eleven million dollars in annual sales, with Pratt & Whitney representing 70 percent of that amount. In 1985 Dexter Tool Company was the second-largest job shop of its type in Florida and one of the outstanding facilities in the United States permitted to manufacture engine parts for the aerospace industry and the government.

Dexter Tool Company headquarters on West Fifty-third Street in West Palm Beach.

SPECTRUM INTERIOR DESIGN AND SPACE PLANNING

Susan Schuyler Smith graduated in 1970 from the College of Architecture and Fine Arts at the University of Florida and became a professional member of the American Society of Interior Designers in 1975. She founded Spectrum Interior Design and Space Planning at the Flagler Center in 1978 and became a professional member of the Institute of Business Designers two years later. In September 1984 she relocated the venture to South Olive Avenue in West Palm Beach and renovated a 25-year-old building. Today Spectrum's award-winning design team provides space planning, interior architecture, interior design, and purchasing skills to clients and architects of commercial and residential properties in south Florida.

Spectrum's commercial clients include medical facilities, condominiums, financial institutions, and accounting and law firms throughout Palm Beach County. Corporate patrons include Photo Electronics Corporation and WPEC-TV in Mangonia Park (1982), the Levitz corporate headquarters in Boca Raton (1985), and Golden Bear, Inc., in North Palm Beach (1985).

Spectrum Interior Design's work was publicly displayed at the 1981 opening of the new City Hall building in West Palm Beach. The firm received an Outstanding Achievement Award in 1982 from the *Institute of Business Designers and Interior Designers* magazine for its creative use of artifacts and historical photographs in the new Central Fire Station in West Palm Beach.

Other interior design projects include Bethesda-by-the-Sea Episcopal Church in Palm Beach (1980), W.G. Lassiter Student Center at Palm Beach Atlantic College in West Palm Beach (1983), and the Colony Hotel in Palm Beach (1984). Notable residential projects include the elegant and uniquely designed homes of Mr.

and Mrs. A. Dreyfoos, Jr., in Palm Beach (1982), Mr. and Mrs. E. Kelm at the Ocean Reef Club in North Key Largo (1983), and Mr. and Mrs. T. Tarone in Palm Beach (1984).

Susan Schuyler Smith has con-

The firm's headquarters on South Olive Avenue in West Palm Beach.

tributed significantly to civic and community growth in Palm Beach County. A director of the Chamber of Commerce of the Palm Beaches since 1981, she became that organization's first female president in 1984. She also served on the national board of directors of Big Brothers/ Big Sisters of America beginning in 1983, and was the founder of Leadership Palm Beach County in 1984.

As president of Spectrum Interior Design and Space Planning, Susan Schuyler Smith leads fourteen talented professionals who have set a standard for exemplary design in the revitalization and growth of Palm Beach County.

Susan Schuyler Smith founded Spectrum Interior Design and Space Planning in 1978.

MONTGOMERY SEARCY & DENNEY, P.A.

The law firm of Montgomery Searcy & Denney, P.A., had its origin in a practice organized about 1915 by Charles Cook Howell in Jacksonville, Florida. For several decades that firm represented interests in Florida banking, industry, and railroads. The firm of Howell, Kirby, Montgomery, Sands and D'Aiuto, located in Jacksonville, consisted of William M. Howell, T. Malcolm Kirby, Robert M. Montgomery, Jr., Lawrence O. Sands, and Leonard N. D'Aiuto, all law graduates of the University of Florida. The firm expanded to offices in Daytona Beach in 1959 and Rockledge in 1961.

Montgomery was the first resident partner in an office established in 1966 in the Pan American Building in West Palm Beach. The parent firm also established offices at Boca Raton and Fort Lauderdale in 1969 and at Orlando in 1970.

During the early 1970s four young attorneys joined the West Palm Beach office, contributing to its development. Lake Lytal, Jr., a West Palm Beach native and graduate of the University of Florida, and Earl L. Denney, Jr., also a graduate of the University of Florida, were joined by Joseph J. Reiter and Christian D. Searcy, both graduates of Stetson University. In 1972 the firm of Howell, Kirby, Montgomery and D'Aiuto opened an office in a new building constructed on Palm Beach Lakes Boulevard in West Palm Beach.

By 1976 the firm was operating offices in Jacksonville, Orlando, Rockledge, Fort Lauderdale, St. Petersburg, and West Palm Beach. That year the West Palm Beach office was reorganized as the litigation firm of Montgomery, Lytal, Reiter, Denney & Searcy, P.A. For the next nine years the firm made important contributions to Florida law in the areas of products liability, personal injury, and wrongful death. In October 1985 the firm became known as Montgomery Searcy & Denney, P.A., continuing the tradition set forth by its founders.

Members of Montgomery Searcy & Denney, P.A., have always taken a leadership role in promoting cultural, civic, and educational organizations in Palm Beach County. The firm also sponsors the Ed Rood Trial Advocacy Chair at the University of Florida and is extremely proud to have the 1986-1987 president of the Academy of Florida Trial Lawyers, Christian D. Searcy, as a senior partner. Robert M. Montgomery's history of stewardship is exemplary. He serves as chairman, board of directors, Palm Beach County Council of the Arts, and is serving as vice-chairman for the creation of the Palm Beach County Center for the Arts. He received the 1986 Philanthropy Award from the Palm Beach Chamber of Commerce for his dedication and concern for the community and its quality of life. Montgomery was named Alumnus of the Year by the *University of Florida Law Review* in 1984.

From left to right are Earl L. Denney, Jr., Christian D. Searcy, and Robert M. Montgomery, Jr.

PALM BEACH MOTOR CARS LIMITED

Formed in December 1979 by Robert Simpson and Norman Gregersen, Palm Beach Motor Cars Limited continues the tradition of providing luxury automobiles to county residents that began over sixty years ago in the old Packard dealership on South Dixie Highway in West Palm Beach. Army Air Corps veteran Robert Simpson joined his father in the automobile business in West Palm Beach in 1946. From 1952 to 1979 Simpson marketed Rolls Royces and other first-class foreign automobiles in south Florida.

Food industry consultant Norman Gregersen and his wife, Sonia, owned and operated a classic Rolls Royce business in Fort Lauderdale from 1973 until 1979. That same year Simpson and the Gregersens formed a partnership to acquire Palm Beach Motor Cars. With eleven employees, in its first year of operation the company grossed over $2.5 million in sales. After five years of tremendous growth, the firm had fifty-one employees and more than twenty million dollars in annual sales.

Joel Samuels began in the Jaguar business in Cleveland, Ohio, in 1967,

The showroom of the dealership on South Dixie Highway in West Palm Beach.

moved to West Palm Beach in 1978, and joined Palm Beach Motor Cars in 1980. First a salesman and later sales manager, Samuels became a partner with Simpson and Gregersen in 1983.

Palm Beach Motor Cars is the franchise dealer for three foreign automobiles: the legendary English Jaguar, the Swedish-engineered Saab, and the hand-crafted English Aston Martin Lagonda. The corporation sells, leases, and services these fine motor cars. Palm Beach Motor Cars also sells previously owned Rolls Royce automobiles.

The busiest time of year is the Palm Beach social season, which lasts from mid-September until mid-June. In 1983 Palm Beach Motor Cars received the annual Dealer of the Year Award from Aston Martin Lagonda. In December 1984 the Florida Region of the Rolls Royce Owners Club presented Robert Simpson and Norman Gregersen an award for their significant achievements in promoting the restoration of classic Rolls Royce automobiles.

Peter Gaydon, (second from left), president of Aston Martin Lagonda, North America Inc., presented the executives of Palm Beach Motor Cars Limited (from left to right), Norm Gregersen, vice-president; Bob Simpson, president; and Joel Samuels, general sales manager, with the Top Aston Martin Dealer in the United States Award in 1983.

165

PALM BEACH ATLANTIC COLLEGE

The concept for a Baptist college in Palm Beach began in 1959, when the Education Commission of the Southern Baptist Convention conducted a study of higher education in Florida. In the spring of 1968 the Palm Lake Baptist Association accepted responsibility and proposed a four-year institution at a location near downtown West Palm Beach. In April the name Palm Beach Atlantic College was adopted, and the school received its certification from the State of Florida.

The college's first president, Dr. Jess Moody, began in facilities vacated by the First Baptist Church of West Palm Beach. Since 1968 a series of acquisitions has expanded the campus to include the E.C. Blomeyer Library in the administration building, the W.G. Lassiter Student Center, and two dozen classroom, dormitory, and support buildings.

The torch of leadership at Palm Beach Atlantic College was passed to Dr. Warner Earle Fusselle in 1972 and to Dr. George R. Borders in 1978. In February 1982 Dr. Claude H. Rhea became the college's fourth president. In November 1984 Dr. John M. Templeton was honored as the first recipient of the Palm Beach

The W.G. Lassiter Student Center at Palm Beach Atlantic College.

Atlantic College Free Enterprise Medal.

PBAC is a private, coeducational liberal arts college accredited by the Southern Association of Colleges and Schools. The baccalaureate degree is offered in thirteen major fields of study. Approximately 70 percent of the students are from Florida, with twenty-two other states and twenty-eight foreign countries also repre-

sented in the student body.

Although the college is affiliated with the Southern Baptist Convention, enrollment is not restricted on the basis of religious faith. PBAC was founded with the conviction that there was a need for a college in the community that would educate the mind while developing the moral character of its students. Palm Beach Atlantic College emphasizes a deep understanding of the American democratic tradition and free-enterprise system within the context of Christian values.

All students attending Palm Beach Atlantic College are required to participate in the unique Workship program. The term "Workship" describes a joining together of two lifetime needs: work and worship. Workship is a part of the philosophy of the college, whose total student body translates Christian concern into action by giving at least 200 hours each of unpaid community service during their four years at PBAC. Completion of Workship is a requirement for graduation from Palm Beach Atlantic College.

Phase 1A of Palm Beach Atlantic College's East Campus is scheduled for completion in 1988.

SPENCER BOAT COMPANY

Melville Evans Spencer settled in the south Florida wilderness in 1875 and became Palm Beach County's first boat builder when he constructed a 26-foot steamboat to tow rafts of lumber across Lake Worth to the construction site of Henry M. Flagler's Royal Poincianna Hotel in Palm Beach in 1894.

After World War II his grandson, Navy veteran Melville Louis Spencer, became a marine carpenter at the Flurry & Crouch boat yard in West Palm Beach. In 1949 he left the yard to found the Spencer Boat Company while working out of the trunk of his car doing free-lance marine repairs. In 1952 Spencer returned and leased space at the old Flurry & Crouch boat yard and gradually purchased the entire yard for his own boat-building business.

Carpentry, electrical, machine, engine, and paint shops were added over the years. The yard was enlarged to include a centerboard well for sailboats, a marine hardware store, and laundry and shower facilities. The yard has a marina, a large covered wet shed, and an enclosed spray-paint building. The Spencer Boat Company covers ten acres, with dock space for ninety-four vessels up to 130 feet in length.

In 1962 the old marine railway was replaced with a 150-ton Syncrolift capable of hauling vessels 100

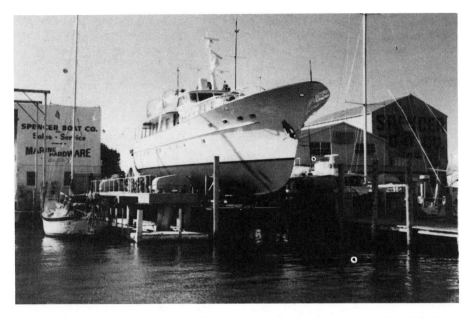

feet in length. Spencer also installed a sixty-ton Travelift and a five-ton Insley crane for mast stepping, rigging, and engine repair.

Upon the unexpected death of Melville Spencer in 1973, his wife, Bertha, assumed management of the company. Upon her retirement in 1981 the firm was purchased by Edward L. Bronstien, Jr., who continues the Palm Beach quality yachting tradition.

In 1984 Spencer Boat Company and Burger Boat Company formed a

A 99-foot Burger yacht being launched after extensive service.

joint venture for sales and service of Burger yachts. In 1985 the yard became an official U.S. Customs Service reporting station for foreign and domestic vessels.

Spencer Boat Company is located 1.25 miles south of the Palm Beach Inlet directly off the Intracoastal Waterway on Lake Worth. The firm has a worldwide reputation for quality craftsmanship and dedication to the repair and restoration of all types of modern and classic boats: wood, steel, aluminum, fiberglass, and ferrocement, both sail and power.

An aerial view of Spencer Boat Company on Lake Worth in West Palm Beach.

GOOD SAMARITAN HOSPITAL

Before 1920 a three-room cottage on Third Street near the FEC Railroad served as an infirmary. Recognizing an urgent need for a community hospital to provide proper facilities for medical and surgical care, a small group of civic-minded Palm Beach residents organized in 1916 as the Good Samaritan Hospital Association to plan for such a facility. The organization purchased land north of Twelfth Street facing Lake Worth. Good Samaritan, Palm Beach County's first hospital, opened in May 1920.

The original Good Samaritan Hospital, designed by architect Marion Sims Wyeth, was a two-story, 35-bed facility constructed in Spanish-revival style. Téresa Fremd, R.N., first director of nursing, assisted Dr. Leon Ashley Peek, first chief of staff, in transporting patients from the cottage by automobile to the new Good Samaritan Hospital.

Continual growth has marked the institution's history. Delphine Dodge Hall, also designed by Wyeth, was added in 1921 as a maternity isolation ward, and the west wing, built in 1925, served as the women's ward and pediatric department, thus in-

creasing bed capacity to ninety-five. In 1923 director of nursing Kathryn R. Gutwald founded the School of Nursing, which showed consistent growth from its first class until it was transferred to Palm Beach Junior College in 1961. Harris Hall, designed by architect Addison Mizner, was built in 1928 as the first nurses' residence. By 1929 the hospital had a busy department of roentgenology (X-ray). Through the years the hospital frequently received generous gifts from philanthropic supporters, making construction of the Shaughnessy Wing and Dillman Pavilion possible. By 1940 bed capacity had increased to 122.

Beginning in 1941 superintendent Earl C.H. Pearson introduced specialization for hospital personnel with the addition of professional admissions, bookkeeping, housekeeping, pharmacy, and medical records departments. In 1945 the Women's Auxiliary of Good Samaritan Hospi-

tal was founded, and twelve years later this volunteer organization presented the institution with a prayer room for patients and visitors of all religious faiths. Funds raised by the auxiliary's activities also financed the emergency room, nursery, gift and coffee shops, and equipment for other departments.

John F. Wymer, Jr., was appointed hospital administrator in 1947 and served in that capacity until 1981.

In the spring of 1948 a $5-million, long-term building program was announced by the board of governors from plans submitted by architect John L. Volk. Improvements in existing facilities happened concurrently with expansion. In 1949 the north and central wings and a new boiler room with a modern laundry were completed. The following year Anna Dodge Maternity Suite became a reality, increasing bed capacity to 150.

In 1952 Elizabeth Golde became Good Samaritan's director of nursing, and that same year private patient rooms were equipped with air conditioning, high-low beds, piped oxygen, soundproofing, and a direct system of patient communication with the nursing stations. Four

Good Samaritan was a newly erected thirty-bed hospital facing Dixie Highway in May 1920.

years later two additional stories were added to the north and central wings.

In 1961 Mae C. Rovensky Nurses' Residence, a five-story building at the corner of Twelfth Street and Olive Avenue, was completed with thirty rental apartments for nurses and professional staff. Harris Hall, unused after the transferring of the School of Nursing in 1961, was remodeled the following year into a 278-seat auditorium, named in honor of William A. Phillips, chairman of the board of directors. Hope L. Stokes, director of nursing since 1963, was succeeded by Mary C. Hayes in 1969.

The five-story south wing was completed in 1962, and a three-story second south wing was added two years later. A new kitchen was opened in December 1965, containing all the modern equipment necessary for the storage and preparation of food. In January 1967, the inten-

sive care unit was opened for the treatment of medical, surgical, and neurological cases, followed in April by the inhalation therapy department for the treatment of heart and lung diseases.

In April 1968 the Richard S. Beinecke Library, designed by John L. Volk, opened at the east end of the north wing to house the medical library originally organized in 1953. A five-story parking garage was constructed in 1970, complete with a rooftop heliport. The William F. Battin Building, designed by architects Wyeth, King and Johnson and completed in May 1970, was built west of the hospital facing Dixie Highway to house the departments of nuclear medicine and physical therapy, and a cancer treatment center.

The $13-million Westward Expansion Program (1973-1979) brought capacity to 326 beds and added 114,515 square feet of floor space, bringing the total area under roof to

The front entrance to Good Samaritan Hospital in West Palm Beach.

over 12.5 acres. Highlights of this expansion were the tripling of space for the emergency room, laboratory, and respiratory therapy department; renovation of the nursery, labor and delivery area, and the pathology department; and remodeling to provide a new surgical intensive care unit, recovery room, and three new operating suites.

Kenneth A. Weda became assistant administrator in 1967 and administrator in October 1981. The cancer treatment center was expanded in 1982, followed the next year by a neonatal intensive care unit. In 1984, the new Weyenberg nurses' residence with forty apartments was completed, and the Rovensky residence was renovated.

Since 1920 Good Samaritan Hospital has been recognized for its nonprofit, nonsectarian, self-supporting health care services to the Palm Beach County community.

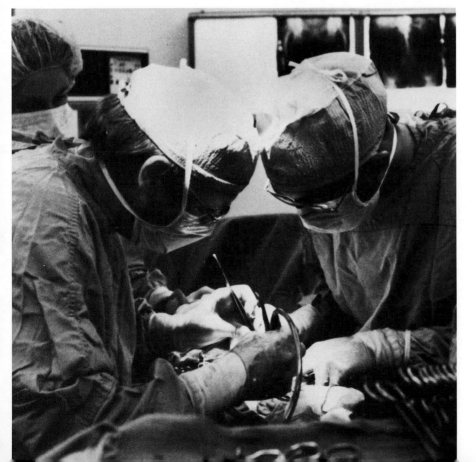

Thirty percent of all surgery done at Good Samaritan Hospital is now performed on an outpatient basis, whereby patients come to the hospital in the morning and return home to their families by day's end.

CONE, WAGNER, NUGENT, JOHNSON, ROTH & ROMANO, P.A.

The law firm of Cone, Wagner, Nugent, Johnson, Roth & Romano, P.A., had its beginnings in a practice formed in 1926 by University of Indiana attorney Newman T. Miller in West Palm Beach. The firm became Miller & Miller in 1940 when Wareing T. Miller, a graduate of the University of Florida, joined his father at offices in the Guaranty Building. Wareing Miller went on to serve as president of the Palm Beach County Bar Association in 1948.

The firm became Miller, Miller & Hewitt in 1950 when Robert S. Hewitt, a graduate of the University of Florida and a municipal judge from 1947 to 1949 in West Palm Beach, joined the firm. Six years lat-er Al J. Cone, a graduate of the University of Florida and a legal scholar, joined the firm.

In 1957 A. Ward Wagner, Jr., and in 1958 William C. Owen, Jr., both graduates of the University of Florida, joined the firm of Miller, Hewitt, Cone, Owen & Wagner at new offices on North Olive Avenue in West Palm Beach. When Hewitt went on

From left to right: John W. Dell, Charles A. Nugent, Jr., Larry Klein, Lealand L. Lovering, Clarence T. Johnson, Jr., Robert R. Johnson, Al J. Cone, William C. Owen, Jr., A. Ward Wagner, Jr., James O'Flarity, and Frank J. McKeown, Jr., on the occasion of the firm's reception in honor of Judge Owen, December 1967.

the bench in 1960, Charles A. Nugent, Jr., a graduate of the University of Miami who served as Palm Beach County solicitor from 1955 to 1959, joined the firm, which became Miller, Cone, Owen, Wagner & Nugent.

Clarence T. Johnson, Jr., a graduate of the University of Florida, joined the firm in 1959 as a resident partner in an office established at Rockledge, created in response to the opening of the Kennedy Space Center. When Johnson went on the bench, the Rockledge office was operated by Lealand L. Lovering and Jere E. Lober in their own partnership.

Robert R. Johnson, a graduate of

From left to right: Fred A. Hazouri, Al J. Cone, Robert R. Johnson, Charles A. Nugent, Jr., Judge Robert S. Hewitt, A. Ward Wagner, and David L. Roth, in 1984.

the University of Miami, joined the firm of Miller, Cone, Owen, Wagner, Nugent & Johnson in 1961. When Owen went on the bench in 1967, Frank J. McKeown, Jr., a graduate of the University of North Carolina, and John W. Dell, a graduate of the University of Notre Dame, became partners in the firm of Cone, Wagner, Nugent, Johnson, McKeown & Dell. In 1969 the old form of partnership was changed to a new form of corporation: the professional association.

Fred A. Hazouri and David L. Roth, both graduates of the University of Florida, joined the association of Cone, Owen, Wagner, Nugent, Johnson, Hazouri & Roth in 1971. Roth served as U.S. Magistrate from

1971 to 1978 and as president of the Palm Beach County Bar Association in 1981-1982. John F. Romano, a graduate of South Texas College of Law, joined the current professional association of Cone, Wagner, Nugent, Johnson, Roth & Romano, P.A., in 1979.

The firm has expanded over the years and at one time operated offices in West Palm Beach, Rockledge, Jupiter/Tequesta, Bell Glade, and Okeechobee. It has been honored by the judicial appointments of for-

mer partners Hewitt, Johnson, Owen, Dell, and Miller.

Cone was elected to the presidency of the Association of Trial Lawyers of America in 1966-1967, as was Wagner in 1975-1976. The Academy of Florida Trial Lawyers also elected Cone as its president in 1961-1962; Hazouri held that same position in 1981-1982. Romano was elected to the academy's board of directors and served from 1980 to 1984. Fellows in the preeminent American College of Trial Lawyers include Cone, Wagner, and Nugent.

In July 1983 Cone, Wagner, Nugent, Johnson, Roth & Romano, P.A., moved to new offices at the Service Center East on Belvedere Road in West Palm Beach.

GUNSTER, YOAKLEY, CRISER & STEWART, P.A.

The law firm of Gunster, Yoakley, Criser & Stewart had its origins in a firm organized by John Kenneth Williamson. Williamson, a graduate of Ohio State University and a prosecuting attorney in Greene County, Ohio, established a law practice in West Palm Beach in 1925 and was the founding attorney for First National Bank in Palm Beach two years later. William Q. Cain, a graduate of the University of Kansas, and M.F. "Buck" Baugher, a graduate of Washington and Lee University, both established law practices in West Palm Beach in 1925. The trio teamed up in 1939 to form the law firm of Williamson, Cain and Baugher with offices in the Harvey Building in West Palm Beach.

In 1941 Raymond C. Alley, a graduate of the University of Minne-

The offices of Gunster, Yoakley, Criser & Stewart, P.A., are in the new Phillips Point building on South Flagler Drive in West Palm Beach.

Past members of the law firm include (clockwise from upper left) J.K. Williamson (1892-1964), one of the founders; Joseph F. Gunster (1894-1979); Marshall M. Criser, retired in 1984; and George W. Hersey III, retired in 1979.

sota, and C. Robert Burns, a graduate of Stetson University, joined the practice, and the firm became known as Williamson, Alley, Baugher and Burns.

Joseph F. Gunster (1894-1979), a graduate of Harvard Law School and practicing attorney in Scranton, Pennsylvania, joined the firm in 1942. That same year the partnership established its first law office in Palm Beach on the second floor of the First National Bank in Palm Beach building.

David S. Yoakley, a graduate of the University of Florida, joined the firm in 1948 and served as the assistant town attorney for Palm Beach from 1954 to 1958.

Marshall M. Criser, a graduate of the University of Florida, joined the firm in 1953 and served as attorney for the Palm Beach County Board of Public Instruction from 1958 to 1964. Four years later Criser was elected president of the Florida Bar, and from 1974 to 1977 he served as chairman of the Florida Board of Regents.

A. Obie Stewart, a graduate of the University of Virginia, joined the firm in 1956 and was a member of the Virginia, Mississippi, and Florida bars. He served as a member of the Florida Board of Bar Examiners from 1977 to 1982. In 1961 the firm became Williamson, Gunster, Yoakley, Criser & Stewart.

George W. Hersey III, a graduate of the Boston University School of Law, joined the firm in 1959 and was a member of the Maine and Florida bars.

John Kenneth Williamson died in 1964, and the firm became Gunster, Yoakley, Criser, Stewart & Hersey.

In 1979, following Hersey's appointment to the Fourth District Court of Appeal, the firm became the current Gunster, Yoakley, Criser & Stewart. Two years later an office was established in Stuart, followed by the opening of an office in Boca Raton in 1983. Marshall M. Criser retired from the firm in 1984 to become the eighth president of the University of Florida. That same year David McIntosh became the firm's first chief executive officer, with the responsibilities of coordinating nonlegal functions in management and marketing. In 1985 Gunster, Yoakley, Criser & Stewart, Palm Beach County's largest law

A view of the dramatic interior of the firm's new office in West Palm Beach.

firm, established offices in the new Phillips Point building on South Flagler Drive in West Palm Beach.

In its early years the firm focused primarily on residential conveyancing and estate work. In the past decade, however, the scope of practice has expanded dramatically to include all aspects of commercial and corporate law. Administratively, the firm is divided into six departments: real estate; litigation; corporate and se-

curities; tax; probate and general practice; and environmental, land use, and administrative law. The firm now serves as general counsel for a large number of regional, state, and national institutional clients and is involved in community and professional activities.

Some of the attorneys affiliated with Gunster, Yoakley, Criser & Stewart, Palm Beach County's largest law firm, meet in the Board Room.

JOHNSTON, SASSER, RANDOLPH AND WEAVER

The law firm of Johnston, Sasser, Randolph and Weaver had its beginnings in a practice established in 1909 by H.L. Bussey. When West Palm Beach was experiencing a real estate expansion in 1924, Bussey was joined by Rufus M. Robbins, a Stetson University graduate and a former Palm Beach County judge, and Harry A. Johnston, a graduate of the University of Florida.

Following the real estate bust of 1925, the practice was moved into the Citizens Bank Building. The following year Henry F. Lilienthal, a graduate of the University of Florida, joined the firm, and its name was changed to Bussey, Johnston and Lilienthal. Following Bussey's death in 1930, Jerome Gedney, an attorney practicing in New York and New Jersey, joined the firm, and the following year the partnership became Gedney, Johnston and Lilienthal. That same year the firm moved to offices in the Harvey Building, where it remained for forty-seven years practicing real estate, probate, and municipal law in the growing Palm Beach County area.

Harry A. Johnston was the Palm Beach County attorney from 1936 to 1940 and a colonel in the U.S. Army during World War II, returning again to hold the office of county attorney from 1946 to 1969. He also served as president of the Palm Beach County Bar Association in 1928 and as state commander of the American Legion in 1937.

Henry F. Lilienthal served as president of the Palm Beach County Bar Association in 1936 and commanded the Civil Air Patrol at Morrison Field in West Palm Beach. In addition, Jerome D. Gedney led a drive to form the Town of Manalapan and was elected its first mayor, serving from 1931 to 1945.

In 1958 Harry A. Johnston II, a graduate of the University of Florida, joined the firm, and following Gedney's death in 1965, the partnership's name was changed to Johnston, Lilienthal and Johnston. Lilienthal retired in 1970. During the next two years Donald J. Sasser and John C. Randolph joined the firm, and in 1975 its name was changed to Johnston, Sasser and Randolph.

In 1978 the firm's offices were moved from the Harvey Building to Okeechobee Boulevard. The following year Herbert Adams Weaver, Jr., a graduate of the University of Florida, became a partner in Johnston, Sasser, Randolph and Weaver.

Harry A. Johnston II, president of the Palm Beach County Bar Association in 1968, was elected to the Florida Senate in November 1974, reelected in 1978 and 1982, and served as president of the Florida Senate in November 1984.

The firm of Johnston, Sasser, Randolph and Weaver was counsel in the formation of the Palm Beach Area Planning Board in 1968 and serves as town counsel for the Town of Gulf Stream, the Town of Palm Beach, the Village of Tequesta, and the Village of Atlantis.

Partner Harry A. Johnston II has served in the Florida Senate since 1974 and was Senate president in 1985 and 1986.

Partners Donald J. Sasser, John C. Randolph, and H. Adams Weaver (left to right).

AMES BENNETT & ASSOCIATES, A.I.A.

Born in Tallahassee, Florida, and raised in Fort Pierce, William Ames Bennett attended the U.S. Naval Academy in Annapolis with the class of 1945. Following a tour of duty with the Navy in World War II, Bennett moved to West Palm Beach and worked as an Army cartographer at Morrison Field. At the suggestion of practicing architects, he entered the University of Florida on the G.I. Bill and graduated with a degree in architecture in February 1950.

Bennett returned again to West Palm Beach and apprenticed for three years with Palm Beach County architects. In 1953 he established his own firm, rented space with the town engineer of Palm Beach, and joined the American Institute of Architects. During his career Bennett has designed numerous public and governmental properties throughout Palm Beach County including Lake Shore High School in Belle Glade (1958), East Lake Junior High School in Pahokee (1966), and the Sugarcane Experiment Station Laboratory building and seedling greenhouses for the U.S. Department of Agriculture in Canal Point (1965).

From 1963 to 1964 Bennett was a partner in a joint-venture design team that produced the master plan and Phase I of Florida Atlantic University in Boca Raton. For the next two years he was also a partner in a joint-venture team that produced Palm Beach International Airport's Terminal Complex in West Palm Beach. From 1967 to 1972 Ames Bennett & Associates contributed to the expansion of William Archer's Royal Palm Plaza in Boca Raton.

Ames Bennett & Associates designed residential properties on El Dorado Lane, as well as the entire Los Incas development, which was designed and constructed in the Regency style of architecture in Palm Beach. Significant large residences designed by Bennett include those of Robert Gordon, John R. Drexel III, H. Tyson Lykes, Austin L. Baker, and Señora Fulgencio Batista. Residences were designed for industrialists Edward Swanson, William F. Price, Henry Ford II, and Ernest A. Steward; sculptor Gloria Novak; designer Harold Schwartz; and artist Orville Bullman. Entertainer Perry Como's residence was also designed by Bennett and constructed on the Loxahatchee River in Jupiter.

Between 1969 and 1972 Ames Bennett & Associates designed the clubhouse and condominium villas at Delray Dunes Golf and Country Club. Bennett also mastered the bureaucratic world of skilled-care health-related facilities, designing 120-bed nursing homes in Lake Worth, Okeechobee, Plantation Key, and Key West.

ROBERT W. GOTTFRIED, INC., BUILDER
MARTHA A. GOTTFRIED, INC., REAL ESTATE BROKER

Robert W. Gottfried moved from New York City to Palm Beach in 1953 and established a successful business for the custom design and construction of houses for the island's wealthy clientele. During the 1960s and 1970s Robert W. Gottfried, Inc., developed and promoted a modern variation of the architectural style known as Regency in the construction of luxury residences in Palm Beach.

Martha A. Schaefer moved from Evansville, Indiana, to Palm Beach in 1968 and worked as a coordinator between clients, attorneys, bankers, architects, builders, and decorators for Gottfried. The couple was married in 1971.

Recognizing the need to develop her own business, Martha obtained a real estate license in 1972 and established Martha A. Gottfried, Inc., in 1975 on Royal Palm Way in Palm Beach. Her real estate firm, which began with one office, herself, and a secretary, now includes an administrative office on Worth Avenue, four sales offices in Palm Beach County, one sales office in New York City, and 100 sales associates.

Robert W. Gottfried, Inc., employs skilled architects, artisans, and craftsmen in the renovation of historic estates and in the construction of modern luxury residences. The firm has an architectural division for designing residential properties in Bermuda, Mediterranean, French Regency, and contemporary architectural styles. The construction division employs electricians, plasterers, and carpenters and retains air-conditioning, roofing, and plumbing contractors. As the business expanded, a marble factory, a mirror factory, a driveway company, and a swimming pool firm were purchased.

In 1978 West Palm Beach attorney Joseph D. Farish, Jr., purchased Los Incas, the former Sanford family estate located on North County Road

in Palm Beach. Robert W. Gottfried, Inc., razed the original 1918 house and constructed a neighborhood of ten Regency-style mansionettes featuring loggias, galleries, and marble architectural elements.

In 1979 Robert Gottfried formed Classic Moulders, a company that designs and manufactures decorative and functional polyurethane architectural artwork. Classic Moulders' staff of architects, engineers, and designers creates authentic reproductions of various stylings of architectural ornamentation previously carved from wood, plaster, or marble. The firm also manufactures moldings, mantels, door casings, cameos, ceiling medallions, sculptured wall tiles, capitals, and bases at its factory on Railroad Avenue in West Palm Beach.

Robert Gottfried purchased the Palm Beach Marble Company on First Street in West Palm Beach in 1980 and installed modern, computerized equipment to process Carrara and travertine marble imported from quarries in Italy. Today the firm manufactures marble capitals, furniture, and architectural elements used in the construction of Gottfried's houses.

In 1984 Robert and Martha Gottfried built a multimillion-dollar luxury mansion overlooking Lake Worth in Palm Beach. Designed by Palm Beach architect John Gosman, the two-tiered structure features solar panels, a Jacuzzi, a complete Nautilus gym, a swimming pool, a beauty shop, a wine cellar, a two-story greenhouse, and underground park-

This residence, built in the French Regency style by Robert W. Gottfried in 1981, is located in Palm Beach.

ing for sixteen automobiles.

As a leading Palm Beach real estate firm, Martha A. Gottfried, Inc., holds exclusive listings on all of the homes built by Robert W. Gottfried, Inc. Martha Gottfried credits their high resale value to the original design and quality construction. Her consistent approach to residential and commercial real estate sales is aggressive and in high style. She was one of the first realtors in Palm Beach to arrange her own advertising to promote luxury homes in the area. The Gottfrieds' contribution to real estate development on the island exemplifies the Palm Beach life-style.

Constructed in 1962, this French Regency-style residence was built by Robert W. Gottfried in Palm Beach.

CORNELIUS, JOHNSON & CLARK, INC.

Cecil "Zeke" Cornelius (1902-1976) founded one of the first independent insurance agencies in West Palm Beach in March 1925. A well-respected businessman, Cornelius was also a community leader, active in the Chamber of Commerce of the Palm Beaches, county commissioners, school board, and the West Palm Beach Fishing Club. During World War II he served in the Civil Air Patrol for coastline defense and later, as an Army Air Force pilot, was instrumental in the decision to locate the Army's Morrison Field in West Palm Beach.

In October 1961 Cornelius was joined by Richard S. Johnson and William C. Clark to form Cornelius, Johnson & Clark Insurance Agency; the firm incorporated in 1962. Johnson, a native of West Palm Beach and a graduate of Duke University, was an insurance agent in the city at that time. Clark, also a native of West Palm Beach, an Army veteran, and a graduate of the University of Florida, had been an insurance agent since 1957.

In 1966 Cornelius, Johnson & Clark acquired the Poston Insurance Agency of Riviera Beach and three years later, the John Turentine Insurance Agency of West Palm Beach. In 1966 CJC acquired the Admiral Insurance Agency and formed an office on Northlake Boulevard in North Palm Beach. In 1983 this office was combined with the West Palm Beach downtown office, giving customers better service through automation and larger staffing capabilities.

In 1977 CJC ventured into Martin County with the acquisition of the C.B. Arbogast Insurance Agency in Stuart, another old-line, traditional south Florida agency founded during the 1920s. The following year the firm further expanded in Martin County with the acquisition of the Tucker Insurance Agency in Hobe

Flagler Center, home of Cornelius, Johnson & Clark, Inc.

Sound. Located only ten miles south of the Stuart office, this agency successfully merged all of its accounts with the Stuart office in 1983.

In June 1978 CJC became the first tenant in Flagler Center on South Flagler Drive, which was designed by architects Peacock and Lewis and built by the W.G. Lassiter Construction Company. Flagler Center was the first major office facility to be erected in downtown West Palm Beach in fifty years.

As Palm Beach County's largest independent insurance agency, representing over thirty of the world's leading insurers, Cornelius, Johnson & Clark, Inc., provides a full range of commercial, marine, and personal insurance. Financial advisors in the life department offer disability income, estate planning, pension planning, employee benefits, and tax-sheltered annuities. For south Florida's building community the firm offers contractor bonds and professional liability insurance.

From left to right are William Clark, Robert Diamond, and Richard Johnson, the firm's upper management.

178

JEWELMASTERS

Herman H. Barr, after a tenure with one of America's first jewelers, Castleberg's of Baltimore, began his own business by supplying diamonds, watches, and fine jewelry to the U.S. Navy in 1911. He also entered the Philadelphia market in 1928 with an elegant store on then-fashionable Chestnut Street. There Barr's jewelers and silversmiths catered to an elite clientele for more than forty years.

Herman H. Barr established a residence in Palm Beach in 1946 and was a founding member of the Palm Beach Country Club. In 1952 the Barr family formed Jewelmasters as a separate company to lease jewelry divisions in major department stores. Barr was an early developer of the chain-store concept that by 1970 had grown to thirteen locations in the Delaware River Valley. Upon the sale of all Barr stores in 1970, Jewelmasters established a factory in New York to manufacture a full line of retail jewelry items.

Josef J. Barr was born into the family jewelry business in Norfolk, Virginia. Upon graduation from the University of Pennsylvania in 1943, he enrolled in the Naval Officers Training Program at Notre Dame. Josef served in the U.S. Navy until November 1945 and then returned to the jewelry business in Philadelphia. In 1960 he became president and chief executive officer.

In 1970 the Barr portion of the business was sold to Zale Jewelry Company. Jewelmasters relocated its factory and jewelry salon and headquarters to Palm Beach in 1972, and during the first year of operations at that site had sales in excess of $4.5 million. Five years later the firm moved to its present location at 125 Worth Avenue in Palm Beach, where it has established a reputation as one of the community's foremost and prestigious jewelers.

In 1981 Jewelmasters' manufac-

Chandelier earrings personally created by Josef J. Barr, president and chief executive officer of Jewelmasters.

turing operation was relocated to a factory on Georgia Avenue in West Palm Beach. Josef Barr takes a personal interest in every phase of the design, manufacture, and marketing of original precious jewelry solely for Jewelmaster salons in the country's finest department stores and specialty shops. In addition, the company has created many fashion trends in the fine jewelry markets and holds numerous trademarks and patents.

Josef Barr and his wife, Corinne, are involved in the elegant Palm Beach social scene and through the years have sponsored several charity events. Since 1976 Jewelmasters has sponsored the annual Palm Beach Town Employees Award. In 1982 the Barrs sponsored one of the Historic Preservation balls at Mar-a-Lago for the Preservation Foundation of Palm Beach. That same year Josef Barr received the Community Service Award, and in 1983 he became a director of the Chamber of Commerce of the Palm Beaches. In 1985 he was appointed to the Advisory Board of St. Mary's Hospital.

Today Jewelmasters has over 700 employees and jewelry sales in excess of forty-five million dollars. Designed and manufactured precious jewelry is sold exclusively at eighty-seven Jewelmasters shops in fine department and specialty stores nationwide, and the firm is assured of steady growth for the future.

This brilliant 65-carat prong-set diamond ensemble exemplifies Jewelmasters' craftsmanship.

FLORIDA ATLANTIC UNIVERSITY

On a sunny Florida day in the fall of 1964, President Lyndon B. Johnson stood on the rough landscape of an abandoned Air Force base in Boca Raton, the southernmost city in Palm Beach County, and dedicated the new Florida Atlantic University. Calling the era "a new revolution in education," he told the crowd of 15,000, "We must not rest until each child has the opportunity to get the kind of education he needs."

That year the doors opened to 800 students, many of whom made the 120-mile round trip commute from Miami to attend the only state university in south Florida. Today over 10,000 students from more than 50 countries attend FAU and get the quality education President Johnson had suggested.

In those early days the 1,250-acre plot of barren land that dwarfed the five buildings on the campus was described by university employees as "like Fort Apache in the old western movies" and "the most primitive place imaginable." They spoke of "great fields of mud" that were "filled with rattlesnakes." Today the land holds 27 buildings that house FAU's six colleges—Business and Public Administration, Education, Engineering, Humanities, Science, and Social Science. A 548-seat theater and a 2,400-seat auditorium showcase cultural events for the enjoyment of FAU students, staff, and area residents.

Not only has the university been important to the more than 34,000 students who have been graduated since 1964, but it also contributed to the development of the city of Boca Raton, once a sleepy agricultural town of 6,000 people that would come alive only during the winter tourist season.

Through the farsightedness and determination of a number of business leaders, the community of Boca Raton, now a city of more than

President Lyndon B. Johnson presides over the dedication of Florida Atlantic University, October 25, 1964.

60,000 residents, has reaped the cultural, academic, business, and financial benefits of having a major educational institution as its focal point.

Thomas F. Fleming, Jr., a University of Florida graduate and Boca

Raton businessman, was one of the first to recognize the potential for a university in the city where he and his family had owned land for many years.

In 1955, shortly after the State Board of Control had agreed to the establishment of a university on Florida's Gold Coast, Fleming helped lobby to put the new school on the old air base land. He not only had to convince the city commission, the board of regents, and the state cabinet that a university would benefit the community, but also persuade the federal government to donate its Air Force base.

After all approvals were received by 1961, Fleming raised money from private sources in the community to help finance the project. Dedicated people like Fleming, who died in 1976, have become involved as donors and maintain their interest and support. The Florida Atlantic University Foundation continues today as the fund-raising arm of the university to ensure excellence in its academic programs.

Students relax in a courtyard on the campus of Florida Atlantic University in Boca Raton.

DYCOM INDUSTRIES, INC.

Founded by Floyd Younkin, Mobile Home Dynamics, Inc., was incorporated in August 1969 to sell mobile and modular homes, develop mobile home parks, and acquire real estate for development. The firm discontinued its sales operations in 1973, and sold its mobile home parks by 1978 and all of its real estate holdings by 1979. From 1979 to 1982 the company was inactive as an operating business.

With no active business, the firm's new direction was determined to be telecommunications and utility services. Thomas R. Pledger, a local business executive for many years, was selected to pursue the firm's new direction, and in 1981 he became a director. The following year the company changed its name to Dycom Industries, Inc. During that time Pledger engineered the firm's shift from its previous line of business into the telecommunications and utility services business. In January 1984

Dycom Industries, Inc., provides engineering, installation, and maintenance services to the telecommunications and utilities industries nationwide.

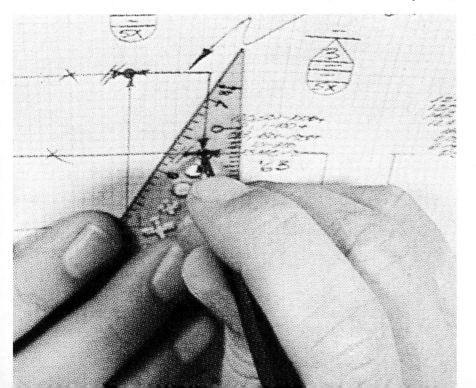

Pledger became Dycom Industries' president and chief executive officer.

Under Pledger's leadership, Southeastern Electric Construction, Inc., of Tampa was acquired in November 1982 by Dycom Industries. SEEC is engaged in electrical utility construction and industrial and commercial electrical contracting. SEEC's services include installation of aerial transmission and distribution systems, electrical substations and switchyards, underground high-voltage distribution systems, individual and commercial electrical systems, traffic signal systems, and street lighting for public highways. Later in December of the same year, Dycom acquired Signal Construction Company, Inc., of Jupiter. SCC installs and maintains traffic signal systems, bridge electrical systems, and highway, navigation, and airport lighting.

The corporation acquired Coastal Plains, Inc., of Jupiter in January 1984. Coastal Plains operates nationwide and specializes in fiber-optic telephone systems for major telecommunications companies including AT&T, GTE Sprint, MCI, and other leading companies. In October 1984 STS, Inc., an Orlando-based company that provides engineering, installation, and maintenance services nationwide to the telecommunications industry, was acquired.

Dycom Industries, Inc., a telecommunications and utility service holding company, has its executive offices at the Reflections Office Centre in West Palm Beach. It is one of the fastest-growing businesses of its type in the nation.

BANK OF PAHOKEE

The Bank of Pahokee's main lobby at the office in Pahokee reflects the newest innovations in banking design. Recently renovated, the bank's spacious lobby is oriented for customer convenience.

The Bank of Pahokee was established in May 1922 with capital stock of $15,000 by a group of enterprising Pahokee farmers and businessmen as the first commercial bank for the Everglades agricultural area of Palm Beach County. The first board of directors included R.W. Windham, Homer Vivian, Ira York, D.E. Austin, and Dr. D.S. Spooner. Windham was the institution's first president and E.G. Kilpatrick, Jr., was the first cashier.

The new bank opened in a corner of W.J. Larrimore's store with an old wire-grilled teller's counter, a stand-up bookkeeper's desk, and a large iron safe. However, the store was destroyed by fire on October 20, 1927, along with George McCarty's post office and York's two-story residence and store. Following the fire, the bank was rebuilt at its present location on the northeast corner of First Street and East Lake Avenue.

During the Depression the Bank of Pahokee was the only Palm Beach County bank that kept its doors open as a holding institution for cash by its local depositors. Surviving the Depression, the institution continued to build on its established reputation as a farmer's and merchant's bank, dedicated to administering to the financial needs of the area's agricultural economy.

The Bank of Pahokee grew with the agricultural area by providing financial services to pioneer bean growers who pushed back the dense undergrowth and custard apple trees along the southeastern edge of Lake Okeechobee, clearing new farmland. Later the institution played an important role as bean growing gave way to cattle and winter vegetable production.

In 1936 Harry M. McIntosh, Sr., a veteran banker from Panama City, purchased a controlling interest in the institution and served as its president until his death in 1961. During his tenure the Bank of Pahokee earned a reputation for catering to the specialized agricultural banking needs important to the development of the economy of the Lake Okeechobee area. McIntosh was a friend of the small farmer and is fondly referred to as the father of banking in the Glades.

The Bank of Pahokee's new air-conditioned home office was opened at 104 South Lake Avenue on May 30, 1949. In the years that followed, the institution kept pace with Palm Beach County's changing agricultural emphasis on the production of sugar cane.

Upon the death of McIntosh in 1961, Rupert Mock, Sr., a veteran bank officer, became president of the institution. In 1962 total assets exceeded ten million dollars for the first time, and the following year the bank embarked upon an expansion program. Following the Florida legislature's approval of branch banking, the Bank of Pahokee's Belle Glade branch was opened in 1979 at 800 South Main Street in a modern facility offering full services to area customers.

Julius T. Moon, a native of La-Belle, joined the bank in July 1947. He became president of the institution in June 1979 and chairman of

By 1930 the Bank of Pahokee had its own building, a new structure in the middle of Pahokee at the corner of Main Street and Lake Avenue, the city's square. Pahokee was the focal point of finance and commerce of the pre-World War II era in the Everglades.

The Bank of Pahokee, the only commercial bank in the area at the time, was the focal point of the young Pahokee community in 1922. Florida Governor John W. Martin, shown fourth from left, and members of the state's Internal Improvements Board visited the area in the summer of 1922 to inspect drainage work being done by the state and local agricultural interests bordering Lake Okeechobee. The photograph marking the visit was taken in front of the new bank, which had opened the preceding March.

the board in March 1981. Moon was a principal figure in the building of Pahokee's Everglades Memorial Hospital, which was the first accredited hospital in the Glades. He is a past director of the Community Bankers of Florida, an association of independent banks. He was twice president of Pahokee's Rotary Club.

In September 1983 the Bank of Pahokee became a charter member of the independent Banker's Bank of Florida, a trade organization of independent commercial bankers. Moon was instrumental in forming the new organization, headquartered in Orlando, and was elected as the first chairman of its twenty-member char-

ter board of directors.

The institution's Pahokee and Belle Glade locations introduced automated twenty-hour banking services in the fall of 1981. For the first time Bank of Pahokee customers could obtain cash and other banking services with fully automated customer-controlled access to personal checking and savings accounts. At the end of 1981 the bank listed assets in excess of $31.8 million. The following year an Agricultural Lending Department was created.

Holding assets of more than fifty million dollars, the Bank of Pahokee was recognized as one of the nation's strongest banks by a leading bank authority. As Palm Beach County's oldest financial institution, the Bank of Pahokee has retained its local identity as a home-owned, home-operated, independent bank with offices in Pahokee and Belle Glade.

The late Harry M. McIntosh, Sr., became known as the father of modern banking in the Everglades after he purchased control of the Bank of Pahokee in 1936. McIntosh served as president of the bank until his death in 1961.

Bank of Pahokee president Julius T. Moon and Jill Pitts, loan department administrative officer, demonstrate a 1920-vintage safe thought to be the first used by the Bank of Pahokee. The safe has been refurbished and is on permanent display in the lobby of the bank's main office.

183

B.D. COLE, INC.

Bertram Dudley Cole, Sr. (1876-1944), formerly with the National Union Fire Insurance Company of Pittsburgh, Pennsylvania, settled in West Palm Beach in 1919 and purchased the insurance department of a real estate agency on Clematis Street. As president of the West Palm Beach Chamber of Commerce, Cole was instrumental in extending both telephone service and the cross-state highway, SR-80, into the western towns of Palm Beach County. He also helped bring the Seaboard Air Line Railway, on its cross-state extension from Tampa, through the rich agricultural areas of the county and into West Palm Beach. He also served as chairman of the Southern Boulevard Bridge District Commission linking West Palm Beach to Palm Beach.

Cole's civic interests included serving as president of the Rotary Club, president of the YMCA, and chairman of the Palm Beach County chapter of the American Red Cross.

B.D. Cole's fleet of automobiles in 1931.

A 1952 advertisement in the Palm Beach Daily News depicted the insurance firm's philosophy of growth through change.

ITERSECTION OF CLEMATIS

ONG AGO...

You can see the change between the Clematis Street of yesterday and today! Usually, everything changes for the better. In the case of insurance, that is a definite fact. Insurance of today gives you more complete protection at **lower cost!** B. D. Cole, Inc., has been writing all forms of insurance since 1919. They stand as one of the foremost insurance underwriters in this area. Representing some of the oldest and most reliable insurance companies in the United States, B. D. Cole, Inc., will insure you with comprehensive coverage against practically all risks.

218
B.D. COLE INC.

P B Daily News
1-27-52

"Constant Service
Since 1919"

INSURANCE
CONSTANT
SERVICE
B.D.COLE INC.

He was a charter member and president of the Tuscawilla Club, an executive committee member of the Palm Beach Airport Association, and an organizer and treasurer of the West Palm Beach Country Club.

One of his most profound challenges occurred following the devastating 1928 hurricane in Palm Beach County. Especially hard hit was the Glades area adjacent to Lake Okeechobee. Adjustments covering more than 1,400 losses were handled by the firm within a few weeks, and that quick action bolstered its reputation for constant service.

B.D. Cole, Sr., served as director of the Florida Association of Insurance Agents and the Insurance Board of the Palm Beaches. In 1931 he authored *The Autobiography of a Successful Insurance Agency,* which was endorsed by the Insurance Institute of America as a handbook on insurance agency management. He served as president of the Florida Discount Corporation and was also the first president of the Palm Beach Building and Loan Association,

which later changed its name to First Federal Savings and Loan Association of West Palm Beach.

The agency occupied three separate locations on South Olive Avenue until 1956, when its first building was constructed at 1118 South Olive Avenue.

The firm also built and operated an office in Belle Glade from 1935 until 1980. Through the years B.D. Cole, Inc., modernized its approach to writing insurance and expanded its operations to include risk management counseling, estate planning, and multiperil and excess liability coverage. Since 1919 the firm has represented U.S. Fidelity & Guaranty Company of Baltimore and, since 1932, the Chubb Group of New York City.

B.D. Cole's grandson, Joseph H. Cole, Jr., was born in West Palm Beach and joined the firm in June 1960, becoming its third president in 1971. In 1978 B.D. Cole, Inc., moved from South Olive Avenue to new offices on Palm Beach Lakes Boulevard. In April 1984 Joseph H. Cole, Jr., became chairman of Cole Associates, Inc., a syndicate member of the Insurance Exchange of the America's, Inc., headquartered in Miami.

ROOD LANDSCAPE COMPANY, INC.

Mr. and Mrs. Roy S. Rood

Roy S. Rood, one of eleven children of Homer H. and Sophia Hetzel Rood, was born in Rood, Florida, in 1918. The family operated a plumosa fern nursery at their home on County Line Road in Jupiter. After Roy S. Rood's World War II tour of duty in the Navy, he formed Rood Landscape Company, Inc., with John Bendross as the first employee. The pair converted a surplus Army truck into a dump truck to haul sand and gravel for cement block and fill for new home construction in Jupiter, Juno, and Jupiter Island. Rood later converted the truck into a tree crane and helped with restoration work following the 1949 hurricane.

The company's landscape business flourished, and in 1950 Rood built his first office on the family farm. Landscaping jobs took him to Vero Beach, Stuart, and estates on Jupiter Island. In 1954 Rood landscaped the eight-acre Jupiter Inlet Colony for its founder, Charles P. Martyn. Rood Landscape Company has also designed and/or planted the grounds of various homes in Waterway Village, Tequesta Country Club, the Hunt Club, Seminole Golf Club, Lost Tree Village, and Jonathan's Landing.

As the business grew it evolved into several divisions: nursery, landscape sales and design, landscape construction, and maintenance. Rood opened a garden center on County Line Road in 1980. Landscaping for individual estates on Jupiter Island, Juno Beach, and Palm Beach was also designed and maintained by the firm. In 1974 Rood became president and principal owner of the 33-acre Riverside Memorial Park, which incorporated the old Jupiter Cemetery of 2.5 acres, now called the Pioneer Section.

Roy S. Rood's professional and civic contributions to the growth of Palm Beach County are significant. From 1947 to 1955 he served as a director of the Resources Development Board of Palm Beach County. From 1948 to 1968 he was director of the South Florida Fair and Exposition. Rood was a charter member and first commander of Rood-Williams American Legion Post No. 271, Jupiter, in

1947. Rood was elected to serve for three terms on the board of the Jupiter Inlet District and was secretary/treasurer from 1948 to 1960. He was also a charter member in 1954 and past president in 1955 of the Kiwanis Club of Jupiter-Tequesta and lieutenant governor of the 13th Division in 1971. Rood was a charter member of the Palm Beach North Camp of The Gideons International and served as president from 1984 to 1986.

On a professional level, Rood was a charter member in 1952 and past president in 1959 of the Florida Nurserymen and Growers Association. In 1963 he was a founding board member of the First Marine National Bank & Trust Company of Jupiter-Tequesta and a founding board member of the Jupiter Christian School. In May 1966 the Palm Beach County Bar Association presented its coveted Liberty Bell Award to Roy S. Rood.

Today with ninety employees, Rood Landscape Company, Inc., continues a tradition of providing quality landscaping services to Palm Beach County and Martin County residents.

NORTHWOOD INSTITUTE

Northwood Institute is an accredited coeducational, nonprofit, private business management college offering associate and bachelor degrees. Northwood has three campuses: in Michigan, Texas, and Florida. In addition to its educational offerings, the institution has the Alden B. Dow Creativity Center, dedicated in 1982 on the Michigan campus to preserve the architectural concepts and philosophy of Alden B. Dow (1904-1983), and the Margaret Chase Smith Library Center, dedicated in 1978 in Skowhegan, Maine. The center is a private library for researchers and educators, and government, business and industrial leaders interested in the compatible, constructive coexistence of government and the private sector.

Northwood Institute was founded in 1959 in Alma, Michigan, by Drs. Arthur E. Turner and R. Gary Stauffer, who envisioned a college that would offer practical career skills melded with solid business principles, ally itself in concept and practice in all areas with a free-enterprise philosophy, and commit it-

Left to right: John H. Haynie, dean of the Florida campus; John H. Hekman, vice-president of the college/executive officer of the Florida campus; Carol Roberts, mayor of West Palm Beach; Dr. David E. Fry, president and chief executive officer of the college; and Edgar A. Madden, vice-president of the college/academics at the Convocation in September 1985. Photograph by Maximilian Kaufmann

The Johann M. and Arthur E. Turner Education Center at Northwood Institute.

self to a partnership between business and the arts. In 1962 the young college moved its operation to Midland, Michigan, on a 269-acre campus designed by Alden B. Dow on the shores of the Tittabawasee River. The institute opened a second campus in 1966 in Cedar Hill, Texas.

In the mid-1970s, Dr. Turner established a residence in Palm Beach County. A Palm Beach chapter of Northwood's National Women's Board was formed in 1975 to create interest in and to support the institute's educational programs. In 1978, through a partial gift from the family of Charles A. Dubois, the college acquired eighty acres on North Military Trail in West Palm Beach for a conference center. Construction of the center was provided for by funds from the estate of Kathleen Dalby and opened in March 1982 as the Dalby Commons with meeting rooms, a well-equipped kitchen, and offices.

Northwood Institute made a commitment in 1983 to create its third college campus at the West Palm Beach site. The Dalby Commons was converted for classroom and library use and instruction began in March 1984. The Northwood degree structure allows students to graduate after two years with an associate degree in a specific management area, such as accounting, automotive marketing,

business management, computer science management, fashion merchandising, and hotel and restaurant management available at the various campuses. Students may also elect to graduate in four years with a bachelor's degree in business administration in major fields of instruction that include accounting, computer science, economics, management, and marketing.

In June 1982 Dr. David E. Fry was named president and chief executive officer of Northwood Institute, and in January 1984 John H. Hekman, vice-president of the college, was appointed Florida executive officer. The institute's annual Outstanding Business Leaders Awards are presented each year to a number of deserving individuals including John J. Brogan (1981), Wally Findlay (1984), Dr. Aldo Gucci (1984), Leo A. Vecellio, Sr. (1984), and Arthur Burck (1985) to recognize Palm Beach County leaders in the American enterprise system.

Major gifts from Mr. and Mrs. Peter C. Cook and the family of Alden B. Dow enabled groundbreaking in November 1985 for the Johann M. and Arthur E. Turner Education Center. The Turner Center, a $4-million, two-story structure designed by the architectural firm of Dow, Howell, Gilmore Associates, Inc., contains classrooms, a state-of-the-art library, art gallery, bookstore, chapel, and administrative and faculty offices.

SUGAR CANE GROWERS COOPERATIVE OF FLORIDA

The Sugar Cane Growers Cooperative of Florida, Inc., was chartered as an agricultural marketing association in July 1960 by sixteen representatives of Lake Okeechobee-area vegetable-shipping organizations to join individual efforts into a large cooperative to provide for the harvesting and processing facilities for the production of sugar. In November 1960 the cooperative contracted Dr. Arthur C. Keller of Baton Rouge, Louisiana, to study the feasibility of a cooperative sugar mill. Both the construction of the mill as well as future expansion programs were financed by the Columbia Bank of Cooperatives. The sugar house was engineered by Arkel Engineering Company with Farrel-Abracca as the main contractor.

The Glades Sugar House began operations at Belle Glade in November 1962 with a rated capacity of 6,000 tons of sugar cane per day. During 1962-1963, the first crop year, 943,775 gross tons were ground in 159 crop days from sugar cane harvested on 22,031 acres to produce 77,617 tons of 96° raw sugar and 5,663,678 gallons of molasses. The sugar house was expanded in two stages to a capacity of 12,000 tons of sugar cane per day before the 1975 expansion that increased production

to 18,000 tons per day. Further expansion in 1981 and 1982 increased the capacity to 21,000 tons of cane per day. During the 1984-1985 crop year, 2,630,301 gross tons were ground in 139 crop days from sugar cane harvested on 65,595 acres to produce 280,109 tons of 96° raw sugar and 16,578,441 gallons of molasses.

The cooperative is controlled by a board of directors elected by its member-stockholders, who grow sugar cane on their individual farms. It consists of two operating divisions: The Agricultural Division coordinates the harvesting and hauling of sugar cane to the mill for all members, and the Mill Division manages the complete operation of the mill from the time the sugar cane is delivered until it is processed into raw sugar and by-products.

The Sugar Cane Growers Cooperative is associated with QO Chemicals, Inc., in the operation of an adjoining furfural plant and facilities. Sugar and molasses are marketed through the Florida Sugar Marketing & Terminal Assn., Inc., and the Florida Molasses Exchange, Inc. As a member of the Florida Sugar Cane League, the association works on industrywide concerns such as agricultural research, environmen-

tal quality, governmental affairs, and public education. In 1977 the cooperative joined four other raw sugar producers in Palm Beach County to market sugar and pool resources to provide for a deep-water shipping terminal at the Port of Palm Beach, which began operations in January 1979.

George H. Wedgworth, a graduate of Michigan State University with a degree in agricultural engineering in 1950, became the cooperative's president in 1961. Wedgworth has led a successful team of Native Americans and Cuban Americans to manage the largest cane sugar mill in the United States. The Sugar Cane Growers Cooperative of Florida is owned by fifty-three grower-members and employs over 2,700 persons in the mill and fields. The contribution of these growers and their cooperative to the economy of Palm Beach County—by providing greater stability to agricultural income and more stable employment than previously provided by vegetable production—has had a positive effect on the area.

The Glades Sugar House of the Sugar Cane Growers Cooperative of Florida at Belle Glade.

LANTANA BOATYARD, INC.

Elliott R. Donnelley came from Chicago to Palm Beach County in 1965 to purchase Lake Worth Marine on the Intracoastal Waterway thirteen miles south of the Port of Palm Beach, just off North Dixie Highway in Lantana. Renamed the Lantana Boatyard, Inc., the ten-acre site was altered to accommodate a 150-ton Syncrolift that was in operation by January 1967. A main fabrication shop was erected and opened in March 1967 for hull construction and major boat repairs.

Lantana Boatyard soon gained a reputation in marine aluminum fabrication of large ocean yachts. Naval architect Jack B. Hargrave designed the 68-foot aluminum yacht *Ranger*, which was launched in 1967. Naval architect D.J.W. McCarthy's 72-foot luxury yacht *Calypso* was launched from Lantana Boatyard's two years later.

Beginning in 1972 Donnelley's emphasis shifted from yachts to commercial vessels with the manufacture of 65-foot steel hull offshore crew boats, shrimp trawlers, push boats, and 44-foot line-handling boats to service oil supertankers operating in the Caribbean. In 1974 marine craftsmen modified a 65-foot party fishing boat and fitted it with a glass bottom for viewing coral formations and marine life along the Florida Keys.

In 1975 Lantana Boatyard patented an aluminum-hulled vessel called the Cookie Cutter; the firm has since manufactured fifty such vessels. The forward-cutting blades provide the propulsion that can pull a 24-foot Cookie Cutter through aquatic growth, with an eight-foot cutting width, at a constant speed. The U.S. Fish and Wildlife Service uses a Cookie Cutter at the Loxahatchee National Wildlife Refuge in Palm Beach County.

A small oil tanker, the *Krystal Sea,* was constructed in 1978 to ser-

Lantana Boatyard manufactures a 106-foot oceanic patrol craft called the Guardian Class.

vice the Alaskan oil fields. The Presidential yacht, the U.S.S. *Sequoia,* was partly restored at the yard in 1980. Two years later Lantana Boatyard, as a subcontractor to Grumman, delivered a radar-domed military hydrofoil named *Flagstaff II.*

Beginning in 1983 Lantana Boatyard began to manufacture a 106-foot, high-speed oceanic patrol craft called the Guardian Class for interdiction and naval expansion in Third World countries. The yard also fabricates 35-foot river patrol boats, some painted in camouflage colors for military use.

Lantana Boatyard has a qualified staff of experts in various fields, ranging from naval architecture to electrical and mechanical engineering. Capabilities include advanced steel- and aluminum-welding machinery operated by welders certified by the U.S. Coast Guard and the American Bureau of Shipbuilding. Other boatyard facilities include carpentry, electrical, machine and paint shops, and a sandblasting facility. The yard's sixteen-ton crane provides efficient, flexible, and fast-lifting capacity. Lantana Boatyard is one of the country's leading businesses for the design, construction, and maintenance of aluminum and steel boats for an international clientele.

The Cookie Cutter, patented by Lantana Boatyard, moves through aquatic vegetation at Loxahatchee National Wildlife Refuge in Palm Beach County.

FIRST FEDERAL SAVINGS OF THE PALM BEACHES

Since its chartering by the Federal Home Loan Bank in March 1934, First Federal Savings of the Palm Beaches has been an integral part of the growth and development of Palm Beach County. Under the direction of the association's first president, Bertram D. Cole, First Federal closed its first construction loan in 1935 and the first FHA loan in 1937. By 1940 the Big First had provided Palm Beach County home owners with over one million dollars in mortgage financing.

Following Cole's retirement in February 1941, Ronald V. Ware became the institution's second president. He was followed by Calvin W. Campbell in 1942. Recognizing the emerging growth potential of south Florida following World War II, First Federal published the *West Palm Beach Home Owner,* a bimonthly magazine to encourage individual home ownership and promote personal thrift and community improvements. The First Federal Home Improvement Loan Program offered immediate assistance to victims of the 1949 hurricane.

Elijah B. Lee, past president of the

The Wagg Building under construction in 1926. Courtesy, Historical Society of Palm Beach County

West Palm Beach Board of Realtors, became First Federal's fourth president in December 1952. By 1955 the institution's assets exceeded twenty-five million dollars.

In December 1958 H. Loy Anderson, Sr., became president of First Federal and launched its branch banking system on Southern Boulevard (1959) and on Okeechobee Boulevard (1960) in West Palm Beach and in Lake Park (1962). The following year First Federal introduced its first drive-in tellers equipped with remote television facilities on Evernia Street in West Palm Beach. That year total assets surpassed $100 million.

In November 1971 the association's name was changed to First Federal Savings of the Palm Beaches. During the 1970s branch banking was a priority, with offices established in Delray Beach (1971), Boca Raton (1973), Boynton Beach (1973), Lake Worth (1974), Deerfield Beach (1975), and Palm Springs (1975).

H. Elmo Robinson, the current president of First Federal Savings, former mayor of West Palm Beach, and the former president of the Palm Beach County Bar Association, became First Federal's sixth president in September 1975. Four years later total assets exceeded $675 million. Branches were established at Pine Island Ridge (1979), Palm Beach Galleria (1979), Royal Palm Way (1980), Boca Raton West (1981), Delray Beach West (1981), Stuart (1983), and Jupiter (1985).

A complete series of historical articles concerning the people, places, and events noteworthy in Palm Beach County history was sponsored by First Federal Savings of the Palm Beaches. These articles began as an advertising supplement to the Sunday edition of the *Palm Beach Post* in 1977 and continued through June 1985. Copies of these articles are on file with the Historical Society of Palm Beach County.

ROYAL PALM TRAVEL

Susan M. Lehrman came to Palm Beach from Pennsylvania in 1975 as a full-time resident. After studying at the Eastern Airlines Training Center in Miami, she and Robert Conn founded Royal Palm Travel in 1977. Since March 1978 the firm has been under her exclusive ownership. Veteran travel consultant Eric Dobb was general manager of the agency from August 1977 to May 1981 when he was succeeded by Donna Kurty, who is currently manager. Both Dobb and Kurty have been professionally qualified by the Institute of Certified Travel Agents. Royal Palm Travel has grown from three employees in 1977 to a full-time present staff of ten travel agents, who are located at Royal Palm's office on Royal Poinciana Way in Palm Beach.

Royal Palm Travel's major professional service is specializing in foreign independent travel for the unique clientele of the Palm Beach area. These custom-designed itineraries have included rafting in Borneo, trekking the Himalayas, and archaeological expeditions in Egypt, as well as the touring of and staying in French chateaus and English manor houses. The People's Republic of China, the Soviet Union, and the Orient are among the other destinations where Royal Palm can use its in-depth expertise. Arrangements include domestic and foreign airlines, cruise ship companies, railroads, hotels both here and abroad, tour companies when appropriate, and both yacht and airplane charters. Among the special services provided are worldwide restaurant reservations, theater tickets, shopping advice, and personalized scenic itineraries for driving tours (whether self-driven or chauffeured).

Royal Palm Travel experts are knowledgeable about required documents, foreign currency conversion, and import restrictions. The agency

Susan M. Lehrman, president of Royal Palm Travel.

uses a major airline system's computer to determine the most current and economical airfare rates and advises clients of immediate availability. Approximately 80 percent of Royal Palm Travel's business is worldwide touring, with the remaining 20 per-

cent being commercial and domestic leisure travel. The agency also aids in arranging member-sponsored cruises for Palm Beach charity organization benefits, including the American Red Cross, the American Cancer Society, and Planned Parenthood.

President Susan M. Lehrman contributes articles to the firm's quarterly publication, *The Royal Palm Traveler,* which serves as a travel newspaper for Palm Beach County. Her articles feature personal reflections on her worldwide travel experiences. All agents at Royal Palm Travel, in addition to researching travel journals and schedules, continue their education by exploring famous domestic and international locations as well as personally experiencing the various ships and airlines to keep up to date in their recommendations to Royal Palm Travel's sophisticated clientele.

Ten travel agents staff Royal Palm Travel's office on Royal Poinciana Way in Palm Beach.

DOROTHY ENGELS-GULDEN, INC.

Dorothy Engels-Gulden came to Palm Beach County from New York in June 1966, and three years later, while working for Palm Beach architect Eugene Lawrence, obtained her Florida real estate license. Gulden joined the Palm Beach Board of Realtors in 1971 and, in October 1977 she represented the Southern Realty Group in the purchase of Martin Downs, a 2,400-acre residential and commercial subdivision in Stuart, Florida.

As vice-president and sales director of Sun and Surf Properties, Gulden managed the transition of Sun and Surf from luxury rental apartments to condominium ownership between 1977 and 1979. Sun and Surf, built on six acres of land, is located between Sunrise and Sunset avenues on the Atlantic Ocean in Palm Beach. Total sellout then exceeded forty million dollars.

In 1979 Gulden established her own real estate firm, Dorothy Engels-Gulden, Inc., on Sunrise Avenue and joined the Palm Beach Chamber of Commerce. In addition to brokering luxury condominiums and private island residences, the company specializes in commercial-zoned land for development of hotels, shop-

An example of the quality properties Dorothy Engels-Gulden, Inc., represents is The Horizons, a 63,000-square-foot, eight-story business and professional center located in West Palm Beach.

ping centers, and office buildings as well as the purchase and sale of completed commercial buildings. For instance, in 1985 Gulden closed two sophisticated office buildings, L'Pavilion in North Palm Beach and The Horizons in West Palm Beach, totaling 110,000 square feet and approximately twenty million dollars.

In 1983 Gulden received a license from the National Association of Securities Dealers for the purpose of assembling syndications and limited partnerships for real estate invest-

Dorothy Engels-Gulden

ments. That same year she also joined the management board of the Palm Beach branch of the First American Bank and Trust Company, a billion-dollar Florida bank.

Most recently, in 1986, in addition to her own company responsibilities, Gulden has taken the helm as vice-president for the company-owner of Leverett House (by the ocean on Sunset Avenue), a 21-unit, private, luxurious, award-winning apartment building.

The December to May social season in Palm Beach is the busiest time of the year for Gulden's wealthy domestic and international clientele.

As a professional broker, Dorothy Engels-Gulden has marketed more than $250 million in real estate sales in Florida, negotiating with attorneys, bankers, and clients to turn commercial and individual financial portfolios into profitable real estate investments.

BILLY ROGERS CORPORATION

William W. "Billy" Rogers, Sr., moved from Ocala to southeast Florida in 1935 to work as a surveyor for the State Road Department on Highway 27 from South Bay to Miami and on the Overseas Highway in the Florida Keys. Five years later Rogers took a job as a bookkeeper for South Bay Growers and Distributors, and in 1943 formed a partnership with John L. Evans to grow vegetables on sixty acres of rich muckland near South Bay. The Evans and Rogers partnership grew into one of Florida's largest vegetable, sugar cane, and beef cattle operations.

Evans and Rogers soon recognized the need for a central marketing organization to precool and distribute farm produce. In July 1947 the pair joined Charles A. "Mutt" Thomas, James C. Summerlin, and Harry D. Smith to form South Bay Growers, Inc., of which Inman W. Weeks was general manager. Despite a major

storm in 1947 they plowed ahead, harvesting more than 1,000 carloads of winter vegetables during the 1947-1948 season. In 1950 the company financed and constructed a precooler at South Bay for freshly harvested vegetables.

During the 1957-1958 season more than 4,000 carloads, with predominantly celery but also including sweet corn, string beans, peppers, cabbage, carrots, and leafy vegetables, were transported from South Bay. In the 1959-1960 season more than 5,000 carloads were loaded at the Florida East Coast platform, approximately 90 percent of which were grown by Rogers and Thomas. Following the death of John Evans in 1959, Rogers became sole owner of the business, operating it as Billy Rogers Farms.

In 1960 Rogers was directly involved in the formation of the Sugar Cane Growers Cooperative of Florida at Belle Glade, and Billy Rogers

Farms increased sugar cane production for the cooperative venture. By September the firm's holdings included 23,000 acres valued at more than $8.5 million.

In October 1978 Rogers made the decision to incorporate. The solely owned company was known as Rogers Farms, Inc., from October 1978 until 1980, with total assets of over twenty-five million dollars in the form of land, crops, buildings, and machinery. In the 1978-1979 season Rogers Farms harvested 246,656 boxes of bell peppers, 152,516 boxes of green cabbage, and 627,357 boxes of sweet corn. During that same period the firm sold 1,204,881 tons of sugar cane to the Sugar Cane Growers Cooperative of Florida and the

The original partners of South Bay Growers (left to right): James C. Summerlin, John L. Evans, Harry D. Smith, Charles A. "Mutt" Thomas, and Billy Rogers.

Billy Rogers, founder of the Billy Rogers Corporation.

Bean packing at South Bay Growers in the late 1940s.

United States Sugar Corporation. In addition, the Rogers Ranch, the family's 3,900-acre cattle enterprise, sold 2,435 head of cattle during the 1979-1980 season.

When Rogers became ill in 1979, his family became active in managing the company's extensive operations. They eventually negotiated for the sale of all assets to the United States Sugar Corporation of Clewiston, the nation's largest mainland producer of sugar cane. The sale brought to United States Sugar the vegetable growing, packing, and processing facilities of South Bay Growers along with 20,000 acres of vegetables, sugar cane, and cattle land in the Lake Okeechobee area. As a result of the transaction, United States

Sugar also obtained 5,000 head of cattle, farming equipment, and agricultural lease holdings from South Bay Growers. The acquisition of the sugar cane growing land increased the firm's overall sugar production area by 10 percent.

After the sale Rogers and his four children—Laura J., William W. "Billy" Jr., Samuel J., and John L.—created the family-owned Billy Rogers Corporation to grow sugar cane and raise purebred cattle. In October 1980 the firm purchased a 4,400-acre ranch in Osceola and Indian River counties and renamed it the Seven-Lazy-Eleven Ranch. Purebred Beefmasters cattle are raised on the ranch that also serves as a nonhunting wildlife preserve.

Currently Doug Lee, an indispensable employee since 1959, manages the Billy Rogers Corporation, which is headquartered in offices at South Bay. In 1981 sugar cane was harvested from 3,400 acres in Palm Beach County and 1,300 acres in Hendry County and sold to local sugar mills.

From 1963 until 1984 Billy Rogers was a founding director of the Bank of Belle Glade. He also served as a director of the Sugar Cane Growers Cooperative of Florida, the Farm Bureau, the Florida Cattlemen's Association, and the Florida Fruit and Vegetable Association.

VIRGINIA COURTENAY INTERIORS, INC.

Virginia Wesley Courtenay, a native of Chicago, Illinois, was influenced in arts and design by her grandfather, John Schrambeck, an architect and builder, and her father, Albert Wesley, a lamp designer. In 1957 Courtenay received her education in interior design, with an emphasis on avant-garde interiors, from the Art Institute of Chicago. In the summer of 1958 she studied at the Ecole de Beaux Arts in Fountainebleau, France.

In the 1960s Courtenay was associated with a successful design studio in Louisville, Kentucky, where she acquired a knowledge of antiques, offered more traditional interior design services, and gained an appreciation for historic preservation. As her reputation as a designer grew, she was commissioned for a thoroughbred owner's house in Kentucky, the interior of a twin-engine Beechcraft, a town house in Washington, D.C., and an assignment in Bimini where the owner's possessions were transported by ship to the island.

In 1973 Courtenay moved from Kentucky to a Florida-style house in Delray Beach designed by Yale architect Paul Rudolf. In 1976 Virginia Courtenay Interiors, Inc., opened in a showroom on East Atlantic Avenue in Delray Beach. Courtenay became a member of the American Society

Virginia Wesley Courtenay and husband, Erskine H. Courtenay, Jr., at the 1985 ASID state conference.

of Interior Designers in 1975, was named its director in 1977, was elected president (of the Florida South Chapter) in 1984 and reelected in 1985, and was elected to the national board in 1986.

Based on her expertise in the design of historic-house interiors, Courtenay was appointed, in 1980, to a four-member Florida ASID design team to develop a master plan for the renovation of the governor's mansion in Tallahassee. Built in 1957, the mansion was designed in the classic revival style by Palm Beach architects Wyeth, King and Johnson.

Virginia Courtenay Interiors pro-

vides a variety of design services to its well-traveled and knowledgeable south Florida and international clientele. English and French antiques, acquired on buying trips to Europe, are of special interest to Courtenay. She encourages clients to use antiques in blending old artifacts with the life-styles of today. The company's work is featured in the design of private residences, offices, restaurants, private clubs, and condominiums.

Since 1974 Virginia Wesley Courtenay has been involved in the annual OPUS Project, an ASID showcase house, as a charity event for the North Broward Symphony Society. More recently she organized a charity benefit showcase house in Delray Beach for The Haven, featuring the work of local ASID designers. She also serves with the Community Appearance Board of Delray Beach.

In 1985 Courtenay was awarded first prize in the ASID/Wilsonart design competition, which encourages innovative applications utilizing Wilsonart decorative laminates, for a remodeled kitchen in a house at the Royal Palm Yacht Club in Boca Raton. In 1985 the Sandoway Art Gallery was opened in the Virginia Courtenay Interiors, Inc., showroom on East Atlantic Avenue in Delray Beach.

BOCA RATON COMMUNITY HOSPITAL

In 1962 Boca Raton was a city of 10,000 people, and the nearest hospital was twenty to thirty minutes away. The Debbie-Rand Foundation was organized by influential residents who shared the common goal of building an institution to serve the health care needs of this rapidly expanding city in southern Palm Beach County. The Debbie-Rand Memorial Service League was chartered in September 1962 by civic-minded women to raise funds and coordinate volunteer services toward the establishment of a hospital as proposed by the foundation.

By July 1964 the foundation had nearly completed a drive for one million dollars in public support and had retained Frank J. Dawson, a veteran hospital administrator, who persuaded the board of trustees to envision a 104-bed facility. The present site of the hospital, on 25.6 acres on Meadows Road, just south of the FAU campus, was selected and approved by the city commission in January 1965. Ground was broken in No-

vember 1965, and the foundation changed its corporate name to Boca Raton Community Hospital. The league became the official auxiliary to the newly named institution and was the first Florida hospital auxiliary to include male members.

Dawson opened the four-story, 104-bed hospital in July 1967, and within nineteen months the facility received J.C.A.H. accreditation. The first president of the medical staff was John C. Alley, M.D., and the first chief of staff was Walter B. Grennell, M.D. In September 1968 the league constructed a new Thrift Shoppe on hospital grounds, and volunteer members engaged in direct nonprofessional service to the hospital. In 1968 the board announced a $7-million expansion program, and by 1971 six floors were added, with the sixth through eighth floors "shelled-in" for later expansion, providing a ten-story, 250-bed hospital.

In October 1982 Boca Raton Community Hospital reached its planned capacity of 394 beds.

Following the death of Frank J. Dawson in April 1977, Stephen J. Ladika was appointed hospital administrator. By 1977 the remaining floors were completed, and growth of the coronary care, medical intensive care, and surgical intensive care units increased total inpatient capacity to 344 beds. This $17.5-million expansion program added many new services including a Radiation Oncology Department. In addition, the beautiful education center, with its modern 251-seat auditorium, was opened adjacent to the hospital. In October 1982 the hospital reached its planned capacity of 394 beds.

The Debbie-Rand Memorial Pavilion was purchased by the league and dedicated to the institution in June 1984. That same year total funds donated by the league during its 22-year history approached $6.5 million. Boca Raton Community Hospital, a volunteer, nonprofit, acute care general hospital, continues to provide quality health care to the southern Palm Beach County community.

FLAGLER SYSTEM, INC.

The Breakers in Palm Beach.

Henry Morrison Flagler, railroad magnate and co-founder of Standard Oil Company, opened his second Palm Beach hotel in January 1896. The Palm Beach Inn, built on the east side of the island on the Atlantic Ocean, was located across the golf course from Flagler's Royal Poincianna Hotel, which opened in 1894. When the Palm Beach Inn burned in 1903, Flagler built a larger and more elaborate hotel and named it The Breakers, for the sights and sounds of the waves breaking just offshore. Upon completion of the Florida East Coast railroad bridge from West Palm Beach, hotel guests arrived on the island in private railroad cars and were transported to the Royal Poincianna Hotel or to The Breakers by mule-drawn trolley.

The Breakers and its shingle-style beachfront cottages attracted many of America's most famous personalities. However, tragedy struck when a fire broke out in the vast four-story wooden structure on March 18, 1925. Directors of the Florida East Coast Hotel Company, descendants of Flagler's third wife, Mary Lily Kenan, decided to build a fireproof structure on the oceanfront site. The New York architectural firm of Schultze and Weaver was retained to design a new seven-story hotel and landscaping reminiscent of the Italian Renaissance. The Turner Construction Company, employing 1,200 workers, completed the $6-million hotel in just under one year. On December 29, 1926, The Breakers

reopened its doors in time for the winter season.

The Breakers reflects the artistry of the Italian Renaissance. The architectural design of the exterior of the hotel, with its porta-cochere, graceful arches, and twin belvedere towers, was inspired by the famous Villa Medici in Florence. The Florentine fountain in front of the hotel is patterned after one in the Bobli Gardens in Florence. The lobby, with its marble floors, portraits, frescoes, Flemish tapestries, and decorated vaulted ceilings, captures the atmosphere of the Palazzo Carega in Genoa. The lobby overlooks a central courtyard similar to the inner garden of the Villa Sante in Rome. This tranquil courtyard is bordered by north and south loggias leading eastward toward the ocean. To the east of the courtyard is the Mediterranean Ballroom, inspired by the Palazzo Deg'l Imperial in Genoa. The elaborate ceiling in the Gold Room

The Gold Room was used for card playing by hotel guests in the 1930s.

was copied from the Galleria Accademia in Venice. Other outstanding features include the Great Stone Fireplace, the Florentine Dining Room, and the Circle Dining Room, highlighted by a vast Venetian chandelier.

In 1969 Flagler System began a dynamic remodeling and expansion program. The modernization added two five-story oceanfront wings that featured the Venetian Ballroom, the Alcazar Lounge, and the Flagler Boardroom. The total number of air-conditioned guest rooms was increased to 568. To complement the palm-lined Ocean Golf Course and numerous specialty shops, The Breakers Beach Club was constructed on the site of the former casino.

The Breakers, one of the few remaining grand hotels in the nation that reflects the elegance of a past era, was recognized for its outstanding architectural and historical significance in August 1973 when it was listed on the National Register of Historic Places.

Flagler System retained architect John Carl Warnecke to design One North Breakers Row, the modern 88-

Guests arrive at The Breakers through the graceful arches patterned after the Villa Medici in Florence.

unit luxury condominium complex that opened in 1976. Two years later Stayton Addison joined the firm as general manager of The Breakers. In 1981 Addison was appointed president of Flagler System. He was named Florida Hotelier of the Year in 1985.

Currently the Flagler System has two real estate development projects in progress. Two North Breakers Row, a modern 48-unit luxury condominium complex designed by Edward Larrabee Barnes, is under construction adjacent to One North Breakers Row. Breakers West, a 631-acre private residential golf club community of estate houses, cottages, and villas overlooking fairways and waterways, is being built ten miles west of Palm Beach.

The Breakers, One North Breakers Row, Two North Breakers Row, and Breakers West are the four subsidiary units of Flagler System, Inc., in Palm Beach County.

PHOTO ELECTRONICS CORPORATION

Photo Electronics Corporation (PEC) was formed in November 1963, when electrical engineer Alex W. Dreyfoos, Jr., combined his talents with those of mechanical engineer George W. Mergens. First in the basement of the Dreyfoos house in Port Chester, New York, and later in the basement of a church in Byram, Connecticut, the inventors applied their training with transistors, optics, and photography to patent the Video Color Negative Analyzer. The VCNA was a special-purpose color television system used in photographic laboratories for viewing a color negative as a color positive on a television screen to determine how the negative should be printed to obtain optimum quality. It has been marketed worldwide by Eastman Kodak Company.

In 1969 PEC moved from Connecticut and built a VCNA manufacturing plant on Fairfield Drive in West Palm Beach. The company received an Academy Award in 1971 from the Academy of Motion Picture Arts and Sciences for its development of a motion picture version of the VCNA. The following year PEC Color Labs (renamed LaserColor Laboratories in 1978) was formed as

Founders Alex W. Dreyfoos, Jr. (center), and George W. Mergens (right) with original prototype of the Video Color Negative Analyzer (VCNA); and to the left, Robert W. Dreyfoos with the newer Professional Video Analyzing Computer (PVAC), which the firm invented and manufactures and which Eastman Kodak Company markets.

a color-processing laboratory to serve advanced amateur and professional photographers in Palm Beach County as well as nationwide mail-order customers. John D. MacArthur's WEAT-TV, the local ABC television affiliate established in 1955, was purchased by PEC, and the station was moved to the PEC property in 1974 and renamed WPEC-TV.

In 1978, after years of research and development, PEC created the LaserColor Printer, the world's first electronic color photographic printing system for making prints from slides with extremely high color fidelity. A

related technique, LaserColor art prints, provides for artistic expression in the reproduction process.

The Sailfish Marina was formed in 1978, when PEC acquired Bill's Marina and the Sailfish Center on Singer Island. An internationally known sport-fishing resort, The Sailfish Marina is situated on Lake Worth just north of the Palm Beach Inlet, thereby promoting easy access to the Atlantic Ocean.

In September 1982 PEC opened a $2.5-million corporate headquarters adjacent to its manufacturing plant. In addition to corporate offices, the facility includes WPEC-TV, which was named Best Station of the Year in 1983 by *Broadcast Management Engineering,* the industry trade journal.

In 1984 PEC announced replacement of the VCNA with the state-of-the-art Professional Video Analyzing Computer. PVAC is a sophisticated digital image processor featuring simplified self-diagnostic serviceability and stable, accurate, repeatable high-production video analyzer functions for both color negatives and transparencies. PVAC and related equipment are also marketed worldwide by Eastman Kodak Company.

Company founders Dreyfoos and Mergens have contributed significantly to the cultural growth of Palm Beach County. Dreyfoos, a member of the Florida Council of 100, was the founder and first chairman of the Palm Beach County Council of the Arts. He also served as a director and chairman of the Economic Council of Palm Beach County, the Norton Gallery, the Palm Beach Festival, and the Palm Beach Round Table. He has spearheaded efforts to build a performing arts center in Palm Beach County. Mergens had served as a director of the Science Museum, the Boys' Club, and the Better Business Bureau of Palm Beach County.

Photo Electronics Corporation's corporate headquarters includes the WPEC-TV studios, which grew from "modest" beginnings at an earlier site (inset).

BOCA RATON HOTEL AND CLUB

The Boca Raton Hotel and Club is one of the nation's classic resorts. Built in 1925 as the Cloister Inn, the original hotel was designed in the Mediterranean Revival style by noted Palm Beach architect Addison Mizner. The elegant facility was the showcase for Mizner Development Company's plans to transform the small town of Boca Raton into a luxury resort.

The Cloister Inn, with its elegant gardens and courtyards, opened in February 1926 under the management of the Ritz-Carlton hotel system. As a result of the economic bust in Palm Beach County in 1926 and the bankruptcy of Mizner Development Company, the Boca Raton properties were sold the following year to the Spanish River Land Company, headed by Clarence H. Geist.

In 1929 Geist retained the New York architectural firm of Schultze and Weaver to remodel and enlarge the hotel. The firm's plans featured a six-story addition with 300 guest rooms as well as patios, swimming pools, and a cabana club on the beach, north of the Boca Raton Inlet.

Renamed the Boca Raton Club, the hotel reopened for the winter season in 1930 as one of the finest private gentlemen's clubs.

The hotel was occupied by the U.S. Army in May 1942 and used during World War II to billet Army Air Corps radar trainees stationed at the Boca Raton airfield. Hotel and theater owner J. Myer Schine purchased the Boca Raton Club in March 1944 and began an extensive program to refurbish the hotel and grounds and return them to their former elegance.

Arthur Vining Davis, board chairman of ALCOA, purchased the hotel for $22.5 million in March 1956. Two years later Davis formed Arvida Corporation to manage the hotel and develop over 100,000 acres in Dade, Broward, and Palm Beach counties. L. Bert Stephens served as the firm's president and general manager for over two decades, developing a reputation of quality service to a worldwide clientele.

At the championship golf course, originally designed in 1927 and redesigned in 1956, Arvida constructed The Golf Villas in May 1969. A 26-story tower, with 250 guest rooms and a top-floor restaurant, was opened later that year. In 1980 Arvida built the Boca Beach Club at the site of the former Cabana Club. This European-style luxury hotel features 212 guest rooms, 147 cabanas, 2 swimming pools, and numerous facilities for water sports.

Veteran hotelier R. Scott Morrison, Jr., joined the management team in 1980 and became president of the hotel in October 1983. The award-winning Boca Raton Hotel and Club is complete with recreational, sports, dining, meeting, and banquet facilities. The large complex includes The Cloister, The Tower, The Golf Villas, The Boca Beach Club, a convention center, an eighteen-hole championship golf course, tennis courts, a marina with full fishing and boating facilities, and a half-mile-long private beach.

The main entrance to the Boca Raton Hotel and Club. Designed by noted Palm Beach architect Addison Mizner in 1926, the hotel went through several transformations before becoming the award-winning resort complex it is today.

ELLISON GRAPHICS CORP.

Lloyd W. Ellison, an Army veteran and printer from South Carolina, came to work in the Florida printing industry in 1957. In 1972 he founded Ellison Graphics Corp. in a small warehouse on Toney Penna Drive in Jupiter. In its first year of operation, with twelve employees, a two-color press, and three single-color presses, the firm's total sales exceeded $350,000. Early publications included magazines for the professional golf industry. Ellison Graphics soon became the largest full-service commercial printing plant in Palm Beach County.

In 1978 the company relocated to 1400 Indiantown Road and has since expanded its building to 25,000 square feet. Ellison Graphics Corp. is now a subsidiary of Herlin Press, Inc. Herlin Press, Inc., was established

Lloyd W. Ellison, president.

in 1935 in West Haven, Connecticut, and is also a holding company for Advertising Distributors Company, Inc., founded in 1965, and Graphics 3, Inc., founded in 1975.

These four firms cooperate to produce a full range of creative printing, intricate die-cutting designs, and marketing services. Annually since 1978 Ellison Graphics, in conjunction

with Herlin Press, has produced a national award-winning calendar featuring the work of graphic artists. Approximately 80 percent of the firm's production is for Florida clients with the remainder for out-of-state customers. Major commercial accounts include advertising agencies, banks, land developers, and industrial firms.

Ellison Graphics printed Palm Beach County's first "Comprehensive Land Use Plan," published in 1973, and Pratt & Whitney's *Partners in Defense: Twenty-Five Years in Florida,* published in 1983. In addition to annual company reports, the firm also prints brochures, calendars, cards, catalogs, magazines, newsletters, and posters.

In 1980 the company acquired the first sheet-fed, four-color press in Palm Beach County to complement its two-color and single-color presses. In May 1986 a six-color, forty-inch press was added to the firm's equipment list. Other important machinery includes a die-cutting machine, a computer-programmed cutting machine, a hot-glue binding machine, and a saddle-stitch binding machine. By 1984 Ellison Graphics had grown to fifty employees, representing ten printing industry trades, and over $3.5 million in annual sales.

Lloyd W. Ellison has been a member of the Economic Council of the Palm Beaches since 1973. He is also a former director of both the Jupiter-Tequesta Chamber of Commerce and the Printing Industry of Florida. In 1984 Florida Governor Robert Graham appointed Ellison to the coordinating committee for Vocational Education for Region 25. Ellison Graphics Corp. continues to provide complete printing services throughout Florida.

The original location of Ellison Graphics was in this facility at 150 Toney Penna Drive in Jupiter.

In 1978 the firm relocated to this 25,000-square-foot building at 1400 Indiantown Road in the Pennock Industrial Park, Jupiter.

PALM BEACH LINCOLN MERCURY

Bob Cuillo, a graduate of the City College of New York and a former detective with the New York City Police Department, came to Palm Beach County in 1962. He worked in all phases of the automotive business and is currently a multiple dealer with ownership in five automobile franchises in Florida.

In 1974 Cuillo purchased Bill Shaw's Lincoln Mercury, located on 4.5 acres on Okeechobee Boulevard in West Palm Beach, and renamed the dealership Palm Beach Lincoln Mercury. In the dealership's first year of operation, with seventy-nine employees, total sales exceeded $20.5 million. The dealership has received Lincoln Mercury's coveted Total Excellence in Customer Service Award every year since 1974.

Gene Brech, vice-president and general manager, and Bob Lesser, award-winning chairman of the Lincoln Mercury National Parts Dealer Council, have been key employees at Palm Beach Lincoln Mercury since 1974. Other vital employees include Maury Gross, new car department; Charles Wood, award-winning auto body shop manager; and Tony Lombardo, award-winning service manager.

Palm Beach Lincoln Mercury operates one of the largest computerized Ford, Lincoln, and Mercury automobile parts organizations in the nation. Its warehouse stocks over $1.5 million in inventory and supplies Ford Motor Company dealers throughout the southeastern United States.

In 1978 Cuillo joined the board of directors of Pan American Bank in Palm Beach County. He is also a member of both the National and the Florida Automobile Dealers associations. In 1983 Cuillo was elected

Bob Cuillo, president of Palm Beach Lincoln Mercury.

chairman of the Lincoln Mercury Advertising Association and two years later was elected chairman of the National Dealer Council.

In 1984 Palm Beach Lincoln Mercury, with 122 employees, had total sales exceeding $46.5 million. The dealership serves the unique wealthy and international clientele in Palm Beach County and is currently among the top-volume dealers of Lincoln, Mercury, and Merkur automobiles in the United States.

In 1985 Cuillo was elected president of the West Palm Beach chapter of Chaîne des Rôtisseurs, the largest international gourmet society in the world, with headquarters in Paris, France. He is also a member of the Sailfish Club, the Governors Club, and the Palm Beach Yacht Club.

Palm Beach Lincoln Mercury, at Okeechobee Boulevard and Congress Avenue in West Palm Beach.

201

ARVIDA-DISNEY CORPORATION

In 1956 Arthur Vining Davis, board chairman of ALCOA, purchased the Boca Raton Hotel and Club from J. Meyer Schine. Two years later Davis established the Arvida Corporation to manage the hotel and develop over 100,000 acres in Broward, Dade, and Palm Beach counties. In 1959 the firm began construction of its first planned residential community, Royal Palm Yacht and Country Club, on Camino Real. The following year Arvida Corporation began developing a subdivision, Lake Floresta Park, in Boca Raton. In addition, the company donated land for the establishment of Marymount College and St. Andrews School.

In 1961 Brown L. Whatley, president of the Jacksonville-based real estate development and mortgage banking firm of Stockton, Whatley, Davin & Company, became president of Arvida Corporation and directed its SWD management team until 1972. During his tenure, Whatley was a pioneer in the adoption of Florida law permitting condominium ownership.

In 1965, three years after the death of Davis, Penn Central Corporation purchased controlling interest in Arvida. From 1964 to 1970 the firm built five luxury condominium complexes on Lake Boca Raton: Sabal Point (1965), Boca Inlet (1965), Sabal Ridge (1968), Sabal Shores (1970), and Lake House South (1970).

Modernization plans at the Boca Raton Hotel included a 26-story tower and golf villas. In 1969 plans began for Arvida's 1,400-acre resort/residential community at Boca West (sales started in 1975).

Charles E. Cobb, Jr., became president and chief executive officer of Arvida Corporation in March 1972 and established the firm's own management team. Comprehensive master planning is an important element in the success of Arvida's residential

Arthur Vining Davis

communities, including Estancia and Paseos (1975), Timbercreek (1979), Millpond (1979), Town Place (1981), The Addison (1983), Mizner Village (1985), and Broken Sound (1986).

In 1976 the Arvida Park of Commerce, an 800-acre, high-technology-oriented office and industrial park surrounding the 250-acre Broken Sound Golf Club, commenced operations. The following year the Arvida

Executive Center, a 65-acre business community on Glades Road, acquired its first corporate tenant. Consistent with the concept of integrated communities, Arvida developed a neighborhood shopping plaza, Village Square (1978); a 140-acre multifaceted commerce center, Town Center (1979); and the Arvida Financial Plaza (1980) on Glades Road. In 1980 Charles E. Cobb, Jr., became chairman of the board, and two years later John W. Temple became company president.

In the years that followed, the Boca Raton Hotel was again expanded at the original cabana site with construction of the Boca Beach Club in 1980. In 1984 Arvida became a wholly owned subsidiary of the Walt Disney Company, blending the masterful real estate and land planning skills of both Arvida and Disney. A company called the Arvida-Disney Corporation was formed which, through a continuing commitment to innovative planning and quality development, will offer some of the nation's foremost leadership and community, resort, industrial, retail, and leisure time pursuits.

The Arvida balloon, a familiar sight to Florida residents, soars over Boca West.

JFK HOSPITAL

In 1958 Nathan Hunt and Paul Kintz purchased Mulberry Farms and two parcels of land along Lantana Road west of Lake Worth. The following year the pair obtained a state charter to establish the City of Atlantis as an 840-acre residential golf course community.

JFK Hospital was organized as a nonprofit community hospital. The Paul Kintz family donated twenty acres along South Congress Avenue and, following a successful fund-raising campaign, construction on the modern facility was begun in March 1964. The four-story hospital, designed by architect Charles McCauley, opened as a 150-bed health care facility in February 1966. Under the supervision of Betty Sitrach, director of nursing, the first patients were transported to the new JFK Hospital from its predecessor, Lake Worth General Hospital.

In July 1966 James K. Johnson, a graduate of the University of Georgia and the Medical College of the Virginia Graduate School of Hospital Administrators, was appointed the new facility's first administrator. Johnson has gone on to provide twenty years of leadership to both the hospital and the community.

Dr. Sidney Davidson, the institution's first chief of the medical staff, established the Respiratory Therapy Department in 1966 and the Davidson Scholarship Fund in 1967. Dr. Landis Barish, who served as chief of staff from 1968 to 1976, introduced nuclear medicine (1970), cardiac monitors (1972), the Laminar Airflow System (1972), and an Energy Conversion Computer (1974) to the hospital.

In April 1970 construction was begun on the first phase of a $4-million expansion program approved by the

JFK Hospital opened in January 1966.

board of trustees. The new four-story north wing opened in July 1971 and increased bed capacity to 238. An additional two stories were completed in February 1985.

Dr. Ned S. Stevens, chief of staff since 1977, monitored the development of an Arthritis Clinic in 1978, an expansion of the Emergency Room in 1981, and an increase from five to eleven operating rooms in the Surgery Suite in 1983. In 1984 the hospital acquired an ultrafast computer tomography whole-body scanner and a magnetic resonance scanner, and also opened a Post-Anesthesia Care Unit. The following year a Comprehensive Cancer Center, a Diagnostic Breast Center, the Center for Comprehensive Pain Management, and an outpatient Surgicare Center were opened. The Center for Recovery at JFK Hospital includes thirty-six beds for the treatment of alcoholism, drug addiction, and stress-related problems.

Today JFK Hospital is a 333-bed, acute care community hospital that remains current with rapid changes in medical technology in order to provide quality health care to Palm Beach County residents.

Along with the latest in medical technology, the hospital staff is proud of its ability to offer each patient the best possible skills.

FOUNDATION LAND COMPANY

John Donald MacArthur was born in Pittston, Pennsylvania, served in the Canadian Royal Flying Corps in World War I, and later entered the insurance business in Chicago. In 1935 he borrowed $2,500 to acquire the assets of the Bankers Life and Casualty Company. MacArthur went on to successfully manage what became the nation's largest privately held insurance company, which by 1977 listed assets of over one billion dollars.

MacArthur, a colorful financier and entrepreneur, built his fortune first through insurance and later through real estate and development. At one time his holdings included 100,000 acres in Florida, several development firms and shopping centers, paper and pulp companies, commercial properties in New York, several publishing enterprises, hotels, radio and television stations, banks, and twelve insurance firms. Later in life he became one of the world's few self-made billionaires. MacArthur, or "The Skipper" as he was called, conducted business from the Colonnades

Beach Hotel in Palm Beach Shores, where he lived the last twenty years of his life with his wife, Catherine.

In June 1959, with approval from the Florida legislature, MacArthur founded Palm Beach Gardens and began developing 4,000 acres into a planned community. He spared neither detail nor expense in making the development aesthetically pleasing, even to the point of naming its streets after flowers (Gardenia, Lilac, and Holly, among others). MacArthur also preserved several large banyan trees, one in particular weighing over seventy-five tons, and transplanted them at the entrance to the city.

MacArthur knew that a strong employment base was essential to the economy of the area, and he was successful in influencing the Radio Corporation of America to locate a $4-million electronic data-processing plant in Palm Beach Gardens in 1961. MacArthur built golf courses and a multimillion-dollar clubhouse in March 1965 and leased them for use as the national headquarters of

the Professional Golfers Association of America. Subsequently the PGA relocated in February 1973, and the development was renamed the JDM Country Club in 1974.

John MacArthur was one of the three wealthiest men in America at the time of his death, and was sole owner of the nation's largest privately held insurance company. MacArthur died at the age of eighty-one on January 6, 1978, and his wife, Catherine T. MacArthur, died December 15, 1981.

The papers of incorporation by which MacArthur created the John D. and Catherine T. MacArthur Foundation were filed in the state of Illinois in October 1970. In January 1978 the John D. and Catherine T. MacArthur Foundation, headquartered in Chicago, instantly became one of the wealthiest organizations of

John D. MacArthur, founder of the city of Palm Beach Gardens, at his prestigious JDM Country Club. In 1965 it was the national headquarters of the Professional Golfers Association of America.

its kind in the nation.

Bankers Land Company, renamed Foundation Land Company in 1985, was established in June 1980 to coordinate and manage the Florida assets of the MacArthur estate, which included approximately 100,000 acres of mostly undeveloped land as well as resort and recreational facilities, orange groves, and a cattle ranch. Bankers Land Company operated as a wholly owned subsidiary of Bankers Life and Casualty Company, which in turn was held by the MacArthur Foundation.

An analysis of the diverse assets of the foundation and the tax laws and regulations governing foundations proved to be a complicated and time-consuming process. Under federal law the foundation had only five years within which to divest itself of its majority interest in profit-making enterprises. A long and complex program of corporate divestiture began in 1978, and an extension was granted requiring the process to be completed by December 1988.

Palm Beach Gardens Utilities, founded by MacArthur in 1959, was reorganized in 1979 as Seacoast Utilities, Inc., to provide water and sewer service in North Palm Beach, Lake Park, Palm Beach Gardens, Juno, and a large portion of northern Palm Beach County. The insurance operations of Bankers Life and Casualty Company were divested in October 1984 in a cash sale of $382 million ICH Corporation. In 1985, through Foundation Land Company, the firm's real estate division, the MacArthur Foundation divested prime real estate at Frenchman's Creek, which included a 1,300-acre planned unit development on the Intracoastal Waterway, complete

with championship golf courses, clubhouse, and marina, along with an adjacent parcel, Admiral's Cove, a unique 732-acre parcel that features a spectacular series of waterways in Jupiter. The Foundation Land Company's policies will, in a large part, determine the future growth of northern Palm Beach County. Palm Beach County is reported to be one of the most rapidly growing areas in the nation.

The MacArthur Foundation has become a major source of philanthropic support to a variety of fields, including mental health, the creative arts, environmental concerns, international security, and Chicago-area social and cultural institutions. In addition, many Palm Beach County organizations have benefited from the organization's philanthropy. They include Palm Beach Atlantic College, Palm Beach County Community Foundation, St. Mary's Hospital, the American Heart Association, the Animal Rescue League of the Palm Beaches, and the Palm Beach Blood Bank.

The foundation is particularly sensitive to environmental issues. In 1980 it granted eighty-two acres of

undeveloped oceanfront property on Singer Island, valued at $22.1 million, to the state of Florida for the creation of a state park. That parcel, together with an adjoining 263 acres, was sold by the foundation for twenty-three million dollars to the county and state to form the John D. MacArthur Beach State Park. The John D. MacArthur Conservation Corporation was established to assure protection of the ecology and to enforce the perpetual conservation easement. In August 1985 the foundation announced its intention to donate 903 acres of pristine cypress-lined river corridor along the northwest fork of the Loxahatchee River to the Nature Conservancy. The Loxahatchee River is the only subtropical river in the United States to receive national designation as a "wild and scenic" river.

The MacArthur Foundation's grant giving increased from $100,000 in 1978 to $57.19 million just five years later.

The Foundation Land Company, located in the city MacArthur founded, Palm Beach Gardens, inherits the challenge of managing the real estate properties in northern Palm Beach County.

Nicknamed "Banyan Mac," billionaire John D. MacArthur transplanted a graceful 75-ton, 100-year-old Banyan tree to mark the official entrance to Palm Beach Gardens.

JOHN C. CASSIDY AIR CONDITIONING, INC.

John Charles Cassidy, a native of New York City and a 1946 mechanical engineering graduate of the United States Military Academy, served in the U.S. Army until 1954. For the next six years he was a test engineer and later director of new products for the American Car and Foundry Division of ACF Industries. Moving from Pennsylvania in 1960, Cassidy established a permanent residence in Palm Beach. That same year he and two partners formed Central Air Conditioning Company, first located on South County Road and later on Royal Palm Way in Palm Beach. In 1968 the firm, which was renamed John C. Cassidy Air Conditioning, Inc., relocated to West Fern Street in West Palm Beach.

As a director at the Port of Palm Beach from 1968 until 1976, Cassidy's tenure encompassed important growth years during which the port rewrote its original 1915 charter and restructured its revenue base. Under his leadership, the Port of Palm Beach became self-sufficient, operating without the aid of taxpayers' dollars. The port's twenty-year comprehensive plan serves as a policy-making guide for efficient, stable growth and development in every facet of its operations. The present Port District includes approximately 50 percent of Palm Beach County in land area and population.

Cassidy Air Conditioning has renovated the heating and air-conditioning systems in numerous large estates in Palm Beach. Its commercial installations include the Gove Elementary School in Belle Glade (1976); The Corniche, a condominium on Singer Island (1981); the Reflections Center on Clear Lake in West Palm Beach (1983); and the Barnett Center on North Flagler Drive in West Palm Beach (1984). The firm's staff includes four project engineers who custom design residential and commercial heating, cooling, and refrigeration systems throughout Palm Beach County.

Active in many professional and civic organizations, Cassidy is a former president of the Palm Beach Rotary Club and the West Palm Beach Chamber of Commerce. He has also served as director of the Palm Beach Chamber of Commerce, the Palm Beach Tennis Association, Goodwill Industries, the YMCA, and the Associated General Contractors. In 1983 Cassidy was the recipient of the Business Leadership Award from the *Palm Beach Daily News.*

The firm's commercial installations include the Barnett Center on North Flagler Drive in West Palm Beach.

John C. Cassidy, founder of John C. Cassidy Air Conditioning, Inc.